THE BRITISH LIBRARY
DIARY 2007
THE FRONT PAGE

F

FRANCES LINCOLN LIMITED

PUBLISHERS

Frances Lincoln Limited
4 Torriano Mews
Torriano Avenue
London NW5 2RZ
www.franceslincoln.com

The British Library Diary 2007
Published in association with The British Library, London
and the Newspaper Publishers Association
Copyright © Frances Lincoln Limited 2006
Illustrations copyright © the relevant newspapers, 2006

Astronomical information reproduced, with permission,
from data supplied by HM Nautical Almanac Office,
copyright © Council for the Central Laboratory of the
Research Councils.

British Library cataloguing-in-publication data
A catalogue record for this book is available from
The British Library

ISBN 10: 0-7112-2620-2
ISBN 13: 978 -0-7112-2620-3
Printed in China

First Frances Lincoln edition 2006

FRONT COVER A selection of front pages from the
newspaper archives.

TITLE PAGE *The Daily Graphic*, Monday, 14 September 1908:
the wedding of Winston Churchill MP and Clementine Hozier.

BELOW *Daily Express*, Friday, 5 April 1968: the civil rights
leader Martin Luther King is killed by a sniper.

OVERLEAF *News Chronicle*, Tuesday, 2 June 1953: Edmund
Hillary and Sherpa Tensing make the first ascent of Everest.

CALENDAR 2007

JANUARY
M	T	W	T	F	S	S
1	2	3	4	5	6	7
8	9	10	11	12	13	14
15	16	17	18	19	20	21
22	23	24	25	26	27	28
29	30	31				

FEBRUARY
M	T	W	T	F	S	S
			1	2	3	4
5	6	7	8	9	10	11
12	13	14	15	16	17	18
19	20	21	22	23	24	25
26	27	28				

MARCH
M	T	W	T	F	S	S
			1	2	3	4
5	6	7	8	9	10	11
12	13	14	15	16	17	18
19	20	21	22	23	24	25
26	27	28	29	30	31	

APRIL
M	T	W	T	F	S	S
						1
2	3	4	5	6	7	8
9	10	11	12	13	14	15
16	17	18	19	20	21	22
23	24	25	26	27	28	29
30						

MAY
M	T	W	T	F	S	S
	1	2	3	4	5	6
7	8	9	10	11	12	13
14	15	16	17	18	19	20
21	22	23	24	25	26	27
28	29	30	31			

JUNE
M	T	W	T	F	S	S
				1	2	3
4	5	6	7	8	9	10
11	12	13	14	15	16	17
18	19	20	21	22	23	24
25	26	27	28	29	30	

JULY
M	T	W	T	F	S	S
						1
2	3	4	5	6	7	8
9	10	11	12	13	14	15
16	17	18	19	20	21	22
23	24	25	26	27	28	29
30	31					

AUGUST
M	T	W	T	F	S	S
		1	2	3	4	5
6	7	8	9	10	11	12
13	14	15	16	17	18	19
20	21	22	23	24	25	26
27	28	29	30	31		

SEPTEMBER
M	T	W	T	F	S	S
					1	2
3	4	5	6	7	8	9
10	11	12	13	14	15	16
17	18	19	20	21	22	23
24	25	26	27	28	29	30

OCTOBER
M	T	W	T	F	S	S
1	2	3	4	5	6	7
8	9	10	11	12	13	14
15	16	17	18	19	20	21
22	23	24	25	26	27	28
29	30	31				

NOVEMBER
M	T	W	T	F	S	S
			1	2	3	4
5	6	7	8	9	10	11
12	13	14	15	16	17	18
19	20	21	22	23	24	25
26	27	28	29	30		

DECEMBER
M	T	W	T	F	S	S
					1	2
3	4	5	6	7	8	9
10	11	12	13	14	15	16
17	18	19	20	21	22	23
24	25	26	27	28	29	30
31						

CALENDAR 2008

JANUARY
M	T	W	T	F	S	S
	1	2	3	4	5	6
7	8	9	10	11	12	13
14	15	16	17	18	19	20
21	22	23	24	25	26	27
28	29	30	31			

FEBRUARY
M	T	W	T	F	S	S
				1	2	3
4	5	6	7	8	9	10
11	12	13	14	15	16	17
18	19	20	21	22	23	24
25	26	27	28	29		

MARCH
M	T	W	T	F	S	S
					1	2
3	4	5	6	7	8	9
10	11	12	13	14	15	16
17	18	19	20	21	22	23
24	25	26	27	28	29	30
31						

APRIL
M	T	W	T	F	S	S
	1	2	3	4	5	6
7	8	9	10	11	12	13
14	15	16	17	18	19	20
21	22	23	24	25	26	27
28	29	30				

MAY
M	T	W	T	F	S	S
			1	2	3	4
5	6	7	8	9	10	11
12	13	14	15	16	17	18
19	20	21	22	23	24	25
26	27	28	29	30	31	

JUNE
M	T	W	T	F	S	S
						1
2	3	4	5	6	7	8
9	10	11	12	13	14	15
16	17	18	19	20	21	22
23	24	25	26	27	28	29
30						

JULY
M	T	W	T	F	S	S
	1	2	3	4	5	6
7	8	9	10	11	12	13
14	15	16	17	18	19	20
21	22	23	24	25	26	27
28	29	30	31			

AUGUST
M	T	W	T	F	S	S
				1	2	3
4	5	6	7	8	9	10
11	12	13	14	15	16	17
18	19	20	21	22	23	24
25	26	27	28	29	30	31

SEPTEMBER
M	T	W	T	F	S	S
1	2	3	4	5	6	7
8	9	10	11	12	13	14
15	16	17	18	19	20	21
22	23	24	25	26	27	28
29	30					

OCTOBER
M	T	W	T	F	S	S
		1	2	3	4	5
6	7	8	9	10	11	12
13	14	15	16	17	18	19
20	21	22	23	24	25	26
27	28	29	30	31		

NOVEMBER
M	T	W	T	F	S	S
					1	2
3	4	5	6	7	8	9
10	11	12	13	14	15	16
17	18	19	20	21	22	23
24	25	26	27	28	29	30

DECEMBER
M	T	W	T	F	S	S
1	2	3	4	5	6	7
8	9	10	11	12	13	14
15	16	17	18	19	20	21
22	23	24	25	26	27	28
29	30	31				

NEWS CHRONICLE

No. 33,381   TUESDAY, JUNE 2, 1953   PRICE 1½d.

THE QUEEN'S DRESS TODAY *Back Page*

THE CROWNING GLORY: EVEREST IS CLIMBED

Tremendous news for the Queen

HILLARY DOES IT

GLORIOUS Coronation Day news! Everest—Everest the unconquerable — has been conquered. And conquered by men of British blood and breed.

The news came late last night that Edmund Hillary and the Sherpa guide, Tensing, of Colonel Hunt's expedition had climbed to the summit of Earth's highest peak, 29,002 feet high.

Queen Elizabeth the Second, resting on the eve of her crowning, was immediately told that this brightest jewel of courage and endurance had been added to the Crown of British endeavour. It is understood that a message of royal congratulation was sent to the climbers.

Announcers broke into U.S. radio and television programmes last night to relay the news.

Hillary, a 34-year-old New Zealander, and Bhotia Tensing, 38-year-old leader of the Sherpa guides and bearers, are said to have made the final 1,000-foot ascent from Camp Eight on the upper slopes.

The feat was apparently accomplished on Monday. A year ago Bhotia Tensing climbed to within 800 feet of the summit with Raymond Lambert, of the unsuccessful Swiss expedition.

NEWS BY RUNNER

The latest news of the progress of the expedition hitherto—despatched by runner and received in London yesterday—was that the climbers were ready, as soon as the weather was suitable, to set out from Camp Seven, established high on the South Col at about 26,000 feet, to pitch Camp Eight high up near the summit.

David Walker, below, describes how the conquest is likely to have been accomplished.

The two figures are in wind-proof smocks of different colours, double-lined with nylon, and each wears two hoods. Beneath the visors for the eyes peer out on the roof of the world from goggles greased against frosting.

Down to the right lies Tibet and to the left Nepal, while death is a variety of forms, none pleasant, lurks on every side.

At such a height no man can survive without extra oxygen, involving 26lb. of dead weight, when every ounce can count; but at this stage silence must supply what nature will not give. The endurance-time of this oxygen, carried on the back in cylinders, is estimated at five hours.

Hands are lumpy in three sets of gloves: outer gauntlets of windproof cotton enclose mittens made of down. Next to the skin, worn tight, are gloves of silk.

It may be necessary for one or other of the men to look at his watch. This is a major decision because of the intense effort of will that must be followed by the physical distraction. It can take a minute to carryout.

TEN STEPS A MINUTE

Step by step, in Martian clothing, the two figures move forward, dominated by their race against time and the mountain in the slowest of slow motion. Ten steps a minute. Eric Shenston tells me, could be considered satisfactory; five hundred feet an hour is what their leader, Colonel Hunt, was hoping for. The estimates roughly tally.

The boots used for so many weeks in the early stages have been discarded. The pairs now worn are not even waterproof —glacé leather over an inch of kapok with soles of microcellulose rubber—"looking rather like boxing gloves," says Mr. Shipton.

Before setting off from the final Assault Camp on the South

Turn Page Two, Col. 3

The new Elizabethan

EDMUND HILLARY, whose conquest of Everest sets the seal on the new Elizabethan age, is a 34-year-old bee farmer from New Zealand.

He learned his mountaineering in the Alps of the little Dominion and was a pioneer in introducing winter ski-ing there.

Hillary's rugged independence made him one of this expedition's most valuable members long before the final assault.

He and George Lowe, the other New Zealander of the party, were making a three-man climb in the Himalayas when Eric Shipton "took . see expedition arrived in 1951 to choose a route up Everest.

Hillary and Lowe dropped their own project and trailed halfway across the vast range to join them. Shipton was so impressed by their performance that he gave them their places in the Coronation year attempt.

Shipton said last night: "This is splendid. Once the South Col camp was established it seemed there was nothing to stop them, and I have been waiting for the good news."

SMILING, mountain - wise Bhotia Tensing, is the leader of the Sherpa guides and porters who accompanied the expedition.

He is 38 and a veteran of four previous attempts on Everest by the northern route. His Sherpa comrades call him the Tiger.

On May 29 last year Tensing climbed to 28,215 feet with Raymond Lambert of the unsuccessful Swiss expedition before the failure of their oxygen apparatus forced them back.

Tensing's people are a caste of mountain dwellers whose "capital" is Namche Bazar, on the road to Everest. They live by trading with Tibet, Nepal and India.

Malenkov going to the ball

Moscow, Monday — Mr. Malenkov, Russian Prime Minister, will go to a Coronation Ball at the British Embassy in Moscow tomorrow night. With him will be Mr. Molotov, Foreign Minister, and 200 senior officials.

Prophet Vicky

Yesterday's cartoon from Vicky on holiday.

Here the forecast is rain—hail—sun—storm, BUT the crowds are singing in the rain SO—

WHO CARES NOW IF IT SNOWS?

CORONATION DAY FORECAST: Northerly winds, sunny spells, showers with hail and thunder, cold. Mid-day temperature 55 deg.

NEWS CHRONICLE REPORTERS

REPEATED heavy showers lashed the packed campers lining the Royal Way last night—and the temperature dropped 13 degrees in a few hours.

Yet the drenched campers refused to quit for fear of losing their places—and moment by moment the throng grew as 18,000 cars an hour converged on London. And the trains had yet to come. . . .

Thousands of cheering people surrounded the Queen Mother and Princess Margaret as they drove from Buckingham Palace after spending two hours with the Queen in her private apartments—a last visit before the Coronation.

Reinforced police could not clear a way : the car was halted for 15 minutes beside the Victoria Memorial.

The Queen Mother, in a white feathered gown and off-the-face white hat, and Princess Margaret, in a low-cut smoke-blue gown, waved. Motor-cycle police came to the rescue. But a little later more crowds ran from their pitches and blocked the route to Clarence House.

DAMP DANCES IN THE MALL

The Mall looked like a gigantic refugee camp. Over 30,000 people were bedding down along the pavements. Twenty-thousand more were trying to find places.

Thousands sat in puddles of water hanging out their clothes.

Camping up to 12-deep on either side after squatting there all day they were thoroughly soaked by the intermittent storms. But not one gave up his pitch.

Of all ages, from toddlers to over-70s, they sheltered as best they could, some under improvised tents of tarpaulin slung between the trees.

Groups were singing, others dancing in impromptu fancy dress. Quieter parties listened to portable radios or played cards. A chain of mobile cafes issued tea, coffee and buns.

It was the same among the 6,000-7,000 camped out along Whitehall.

They seemed to have thought of everything. If the sun shines today—well, some had brought parasols. If it gets very cold : there were thick blankets and heavy coats.

TENT TOWN

But it was raining a slow, miserable, penetrating drizzle. And from Trafalgar Square to Parliament Square the kerbs were lined with people huddled under tarpaulins, blankets, newspapers, umbrellas—some of them hidden completely and looking rather like a pile of covered bricks; almost inanimate except for an odd rustle of nylon or corduroy from under the edge.

All ages, from five years upwards, they, too, had come with the family.

Even a newsboy outside the House of Commons caught the spirit of the hour, telling the crowd in case they did not want to read a paper, "every copy is waterproof."

As Big Ben boomed eight Whitehall's milkman, 32-year-old James Locke, handed out his 300th pint to the campers. Jimmy Locke, the man who

Turn Page Two. Col. 5

Stabbed girl dead in Thames

A MURDERED girl was found in the Thames yesterday ; and last night the police feared her girl companion had been killed too.

The girl in the river was 16-year-old Barbara Songhurst, a chemist's assistant, of Princes Road, Teddington. She was stabbed three times in the back after being assaulted on Lovers' Towpath at Ham, Surrey.

On Sunday Barbara went cycling with her friend, 18-year-old Christina Reed, of Roy Crescent, Hampton Hill.

See Page Five

400 watch sea rescue

Watched by her 400 passengers, three brothers were taken aboard the Isle of Man steamer Sinnefell from their crippled sailing boat in a storm eight miles off the island yesterday.

The brothers, Christopher, Frank and Ian Whipp, of Rochdale, had ridden the storm, which demanded their sloop for 15 hours.

After the brothers had been taken aboard the steamer in heavy seas Douglas lifeboat took the sloop in tow.

No bread

All those Coronation sandwiches have started a bread famine in London and the suburbs. People yesterday toured from shop to shop in vain.

Said one group of bakeries : "We made half a week's normal supply to sell today. There is no time to bake and distribute more."

Thousands went sight-seeing during the week-end ; thousands decided to take up their positions on Coronation way yesterday instead of this morning ; and thousands more arranged television parties at the last minute. And they all cut deeply into the loaf for sandwiches.

Flash kills 3 cricketers

Lightning struck three cricketers dead at a Coronation match yesterday. The flash shot through the dressing room at Irlam, near Manchester.

The men killed were Ernest Taylor, 44, Herbert Vaudrey, 37, and George Perry, 31, all of Cadishead.

CENTRAL 5000

WEATHER — Showers and short sunny intervals. Midday temp 50-55. Sun rises 4.45 a.m., sets 9.19 p.m. Moon 06.55 a.m.—9.34 a.m. Lights 10.07 p.m.-3.49 a.m. tomorrow. High water at London Bridge 3.48 a.m.-5.54 p.m.

Weather map, Page Two

INTRODUCTION

'You don't know what an exciting business the putting together of a newspaper is. It does not just put itself through the letterbox of its own – the print does not jump on to the page by itself and the pages do not cut and bind themselves alone and the illustrations aren't done on each copy by the artist – the whole process is extremely complicated and skilful and I am always astonished to this day that it can happen at all and at such speed.'

William Makepeace Thackeray, writing about his first visit to *The Standard*

More than a hundred years later, in the 1960s, Cecil King (chief executive of the Mirror Group) declared that by the end of the twentieth century there would be just three daily national newspapers – *The Times*, the *Daily Mail* and the *Daily Mirror*. How wrong he was! Today there are eleven titles and others are planned. Newspapers have seen the ever-growing Internet as not a threat but a challenge, and have embraced it gladly.

The front pages shown in this diary cover a wide range of events from the past century: assassination, exploration, finance, politics, royalty, terrorism, war . . . and from the brash tabloid papers to the more reflective broadsheets they all have a common theme: to present to the reader a story vividly told, and one that will sell newspapers.

But will there be a need for national newspapers in the future? Although there has been a growth in twenty-four-hour news channels on television, as well as the Internet, the short answer is 'Yes'. Rather than sit in front of a static screen, I believe that people will continue to read newspapers which they can carry around and dip into, wherever they are. The format, design and presentation will undoubtedly change, especially so as to catch and retain younger readers; nevertheless there will always be a need for fine writing in newspaper form.

The final words must go to Rupert Murdoch, a major force in today's newspaper world: 'Great journalists will always be needed but the product of their work may not always be on paper – it may ultimately just be [available] electronically. But for many, many, many years to come it will be disseminated on both. There will always be room for good journalism and good reporting. And a need for it, to get the truth out.'

Dennis Griffiths
Author of *Fleet Street: 500 Years of the Press* (The British Library, 2006)

JANUARY

1 MONDAY

New Year's Day
Holiday, UK, Republic of Ireland, Canada, USA, Australia and New Zealand

2 TUESDAY

Holiday, Scotland and New Zealand

3 WEDNESDAY

Full Moon

4 THURSDAY

5 FRIDAY

6 SATURDAY

Epiphany

7 SUNDAY

The Guardian, Saturday, 1 January 2000: the dawn of a new millennium.

1.1.2000

Photograph: Corbis

Dawn of a new millennium

THE INDEPENDENT

No 5,374   www.independent.co.uk   THURSDAY 8 JANUARY 2004   ★★★★ 60p

Revealed: how global warming will cause extinction of a million species

BY STEVE CONNOR
Science Editor

A QUARTER of known land animals and plants, more than a million species, will eventually die out because of the global warming that will take place over the next 50 years, the most important study of its kind has concluded.

International scientists from eight countries have warned that, based even on the most conservative estimates, rising temperatures will trigger a global mass extinction of unprecedented proportions.

They said global warming will set in train a far bigger threat to terrestrial species than previously realised, at least on a par with the already well-documented destruction of natural habitats around the world.

It is the first time such a powerful assessment has been made and its conclusions will shock even those environmentalists accustomed to "worst-case" scenarios.

Professor Chris Thomas, a conservation biologist from Leeds University who led the research team, said only the "immediate" switch to green technologies and the active removal of carbon dioxide from the atmosphere could avert ecological disaster. "It will be a surprise to a lot of people," he said. "For some years scientists have said climate change may lead to some extinctions but until now there's been no numerical analysis of how big this is likely to be. We had no idea of whether it would lead to the extinction of a few species or a really substantial number. This study suggests the latter and it's extremely worrying.

"If the projections can be extrapolated globally, and to other groups of land animals and plants, our analyses suggest that much more than a million species could be threatened with extinction as a result of climate change."

The study, in the journal *Nature*, investigated 1,103 species of plants, mammals, birds, reptiles, frogs, butterflies and other insects living in six areas - Europe, South Africa, Australia, Brazil, Mexico and Costa Rica.

The scientists calculated the effect of rising temperatures on each species using the three future scenarios proposed by the UN's intergovernmental panel on climate change

ENDANGERED BY HUMANKIND

Mexico
Many desert species such as the pocket gopher, left, and the Jico deer mouse are particularly vulnerable to climate change because they have to migrate vast distances in flat regions such as the Chihuahuan desert

Costa Rica
The golden toad, above, and the harlequin frog have not been seen since the late 1980s and are feared to be extinct or nearly extinct in the cloud forests of central America. Worryingly the golden toad became extinct from a protected nature reserve

Mexico
The cape pygmy-owl, restricted to the Sierra de la Laguna mountains at the tip of Baja California

Costa Rica
The harlequin frog has not been seen since 1980s. Feared extinct

Brazil
The entire current distribution of the tree *Virola sebifera* in the Cerrado of Brazil is expected to become climatically unsuitable by 2050. Both climate change and habitat loss are threatening between 33 and 48 per cent of endemic trees in Brazil's natural savannah grasslands

Europe
The azure-winged magpie, found in arid parts of Spain and Portugal: expected range loss up to 95 per cent

Europe
Many birds are threatened by climate change due to the loss of climatically suitable habitats. The red kite could lose up to 86 per cent of its range as a result of warmer temperatures — an additional pressure following centuries of persecution

Europe
The spotless starling, another Iberian species: expected range loss up to 86 per cent

Australia
Boyd's forest dragon, found in the wet tropical region of Queensland: 90 per cent of its range predicted to be unsuitable by 2050

South Africa
The riverine rabbit, left, already one of the world's rarest mammals is now threatened with extinction with other mammals such as the giant golden mole

South Africa
The Cape Floristic Region is one of the six richest plant regions in the world. The toffee-apple comebrush is found in just a few localities and it is predicted that all of them will become climatically unsuitable by 2050 — a major dieback of the plant has already occurred following extensive droughts

Australia
The orange white-spot skipper, an Australian butterfly; of 24 such butterflies studied, 21 face extinction

Estimates for species extinction based on IPCC maximum global average temperature increases of 0.5°C to 3°C by 2050
Extinction risks cover 20 per cent of the Earth's terrestrial surface
Lower-range scenarios predict 18 per cent of species extinct
Mid-range scenarios predict 24 per cent of species extinct
Maximum-change scenarios predict 35 per cent of species extinct

Pictures: Ardea

(IPCC) which has predicted minimum, mid-range and maximum global average temperature increases of between 0.5C to 3C by 2050.

Based on the knowledge of the relatively gradual onset and aftermath of an ice age – and of the past 30 years of dramatically rising temperatures – the scientists were able to assess whether the expected climate change would result in a species shifting to a cooler region, or not.

A warmer world would push most species towards the poles or higher up mountains but for many this would be impossible. The home territories of those that could move might be so reduced as to make a breeding population unviable.

The study found:
● Of Australia's more than 400 butterfly species, of which nearly 200 are unique to the continent, all but three might not survive in the present home ranges. More than half could be wiped out.
● Brazil's unique savannah grassland the Cerrado faces disaster with some 45 per cent of the endemic plants – some 2,000 species – facing extinction.
● In Europe, the study predicts a 25 per cent extinction rate for birds under the maximum temperature scenario of the IPCC.
● In Mexico's Chihuahuan desert, extinction would be particularly high because threatened species would have to travel long distances to reach cooler climates.
● In South Africa's Cape Floristic region, the scientists believe

between 30 and 40 per cent of the Proteaceae, a family of flowering plants that includes South Africa's national flower, the king protea, will die.
● In Costa Rica's Monteverde cloud forests, warmer temperatures would increase the altitude at which clouds form and even prevent their formation.

Lee Hannah, a senior fellow at the Centre for Applied Biodiversity Science at Conservation International in Washington DC, said the combination of habitat loss and global warming would mean that there would be no safe havens even for some of the most-protected species.

"This study makes it clear that climate change is the most significant new threat for extinctions this century," Dr Hannah said. "The combination of increasing habitat loss, already recognised as the largest single threat to species, and climate change, is likely to devastate the ability of species to move and survive."

Leading article, page 16

Blair forced on the defensive over naming of Kelly

TONY BLAIR faced fierce questioning over the David Kelly affair yesterday as Michael Howard, the Tory leader, landed a series of damaging blows about the Prime Minister's role in the unmasking of the government scientist.

Mr Howard deftly exploited the differences between Mr Blair's version – that it was "completely untrue" that he had authorised the naming of Dr Kelly – and that of Sir Kevin Tebbit, permanent secretary at the Ministry of Defence.

Sir Kevin told the Hutton inquiry that the strategy which led to the identification of Dr Kelly was agreed at a meeting chaired by Mr Blair on 8 July, 11 days before the weapons expert committed suicide.

BY ANDREW GRICE
AND KIM SENGUPTA

The clash between revelations that No 10 had written to Lord Hutton two months ago in an apparent attempt to explain the discrepancies, leading to accusations that the Government was trying to influence the report, which Lord Hutton denied yesterday.

Mr Howard said in the Commons: "Either the permanent secretary or the Prime Minister is not telling the truth."

The tough exchanges during Prime Minister's Questions ensure that Mr Blair's role will be under intense scrutiny when Lord Hutton publishes the results of his inquiry later this month. While insisting Mr

Tony Blair: Scrutinised

Howard should wait for the report's publication, he admitted he would have to resign if it was found he had lied.

He also adopted what appeared to be legalistic language when he said: "I stand by

the totality of what I said at the time." His carefully chosen words are believed to refer to the distinction he made then between leaking Dr Kelly's name and confirming his identity "once the name is out" – as the MoD duly did to journalists.

Mr Blair's original remarks were made during a flight in the Far East just after Dr Kelly's death last July.

Tories were buoyed by Mr Howard's confident assurance as he was looking forward to debating the report with Mr Blair, and compared it with the Prime Minister's rather unconvincing reply of "So am I."

Lord Hutton reserved some of the pressure on Mr Blair yesterday by disclosing that the Government was not the only

party to make a final submission to him after he finished taking evidence last October. The law lord said that he also received submissions from the BBC, its journalist Andrew Gilligan and the Kelly family.

Lord Hutton said: "There was nothing surprising or unexpected or of special significance in the making of these written submissions."

Although he wanted the documents to be published, he had decided not to do so, after the parties claimed that would result in trial by media.

It is understood that while the Government tried to explain apparent discrepancies in the accounts given by Mr Blair and Sir Kevin, lawyers for the Kelly family have pointed out

discrepancies in what was said by a wide number of government witnesses about the naming strategy and the "duty of care" exercised by the Ministry of Defence. Mr Gilligan is said to have attempted to explain the circumstances surrounding his communications with members of the Commons Foreign Affairs Committee, in which he revealed that Dr Kelly was a source for the BBC journalist Susan Watts.

After Lord Hutton delivers his report, Dr Kelly's widow Janice will make a statement. Yesterday, her solicitor Peter Jacobsen said: "I am sure that Lord Hutton's report will be scrupulously fair, and he will not let himself be pressurised."

The Kelly affair, page 4

Belgium €3.25; Cyprus €2.60; Egypt £E10.00; France €3.30; Greece €3.60; Hong Kong HK$40.00; Jordan J Dinar 3.70; Netherlands €3.30; Singapore $$9.80; USA $4.40

JANUARY

8 MONDAY

9 TUESDAY

10 WEDNESDAY

11 THURSDAY   Last Quarter

12 FRIDAY

13 SATURDAY

14 SUNDAY

The Independent, Thursday, 8 January 2004: scientists warn of the perils of global warming.

JANUARY

15 MONDAY   *Holiday, USA (Martin Luther King's birthday)*

---

16 TUESDAY

---

17 WEDNESDAY

---

18 THURSDAY

---

19 FRIDAY   New Moon

---

20 SATURDAY   *Islamic New Year (subject to sighting of the moon)*

---

21 SUNDAY

Daily Mirror, Thursday, 17 January 1991: Britain and her allies go to war against Iraq.

DAILY Mirror

Thursday, January 17, 1991 **NEWSPAPER FOR THE NINETIES** Average November sale:3,820,577 (INCORPORATING THE DAILY RECORD) 25p

600 jets in swoop on Saddam

WAR

4am NEWS FLASH

SUDDEN STRIKE: Waves of American warplanes launched a terrifying blitz on Iraq last night, blasting key military targets

Bombers hit Baghdad in Operation Desert Storm

WAR against Iraq erupted last night with devastating air raids on Baghdad and Kuwait.

Six hundred warplanes, including British Tornadoes, launched a five-hour blitz on the Iraqi capital and other key targets.

The Allied offensive to kick Sad-

From BILL AKASS in Saudi, STEWART DICKSON in Washington and DAVID LEIGH in London

dam Hussein out of Kuwait was under way with a vengeance.

Several thousand bombs and 100 cruise missiles blasted Saddam's military sites.

The colossal power of the bombing onslaught was equivalent to two of the atomic bombs dropped at Hiroshima.

But there was no retaliation from the Iraqis — and there were no Allied losses.

All the planes got back

safely, said a Pentagon source.

Saddam Hussein and his top command had been taken by complete surprise.

The Pentagon said that the Allied jets would **INCXREASE** its attacks on Saddam's forces today.

The Allied warplanes howled over the Iraqi capital in waves every 15 minutes, hitting their targets with pin-point accuracy.

Four nations took part in the raid. America's "Wild Weasel" bombers

■ **Turn to Page 2**

GULF BATTLE BEGINS: Pages 2, 3, 4, 5, 6, 7, 20 and 21

LATE LONDON EDITION

DAILY HERALD

To-day's Weather
Wind S.E., light or modera e. Rain early, then fairer temporarily mist. Moderate temperature.

No. 2,488 (No. 1,495—New Series) LONDON, WEDNESDAY, JANUARY 23, 1924. ONE PENNY

FIRST BRITISH LABOUR CABINET

MR. MACDONALD NOW PREMIER

Rapid Developments Follow on Mr. Baldwin's Resignation

AUDIENCES WITH THE KING

Three Peers in the Government: Admiralty Provides a Surprise

The announcement of the constitution of a Labour Cabinet, the first in this country, followed closely, yesterday, on Mr. Baldwin's resignation and Mr. MacDonald's undertaking to form a Government.

The list, which includes the names of three peers (Lords Haldane, Parmoor, and Chelmsford), and three commoners without seats in the House (Mr. Arthur Henderson, Sir Sydney Olivier and Brigadier-General C. B. Thomson), contains many surprises.

The appointments of Ministers not in the Cabinet and Under-Secretaries will be announced later.

A DAY OF QUICK CHANGES

Mr. MacDonald Shows He is Well Prepared

Events in the political world moved yesterday with dramatic suddenness.

In the course of a few hours,

1. Mr. Baldwin tendered his resignation to the King, which was accepted;
2. Mr. Ramsay MacDonald was summoned to Buckingham Palace and signified his willingness to undertake the responsibility of forming a Labour Government;
3. Mr. Baldwin announced his resignation in the House of Commons, and after a brief meeting, Parliament adjourned until February 12.
4. Mr. Ramsay MacDonald, after a second audience with the King, announced the complete constitution of his Cabinet, leaving only a few ministries to be filled.

The allocation of offices to a large extent falsifies most predictions, and contains some names that have hardly even been mentioned as likely to take office.

THE CABINET

The full list is as follows:—

First Lord of the Treasury and Secretary of State for Foreign Affairs, Mr. J. Ramsay MacDonald.

Lord Privy Seal and Deputy Leader of the House of Commons, Mr. J. R. Clynes.

Lord President of the Council, Lord Parmoor.

Lord Chancellor, Viscount Haldane.

Chancellor of the Exchequer, Mr. Philip Snowden.

Home Secretary, Mr. Arthur Henderson.

Colonial Secretary, Mr. J. H. Thomas.

Secretary for War, Mr. Stephen Walsh.

Secretary for India, Sir Sydney Olivier.

Secretary for Air, Brig.-Gen. C. B. Thomson.

First Lord of the Admiralty, Viscount Chelmsford.

President of the Board of Trade, Mr. Sidney Webb.

Minister of Health, Mr. John Wheatley.

Minister of Agriculture and Fisheries, Mr. Noel Buxton.

Secretary for Scotland, Mr. William Adamson.

President of the Board of Education, Mr. Charles P. Trevelyan.

Minister of Labour, Mr. Thomas Shaw.

Postmaster-General, Mr. Vernon Hartshorn.

Chancellor of the Duchy of Lancaster, Colonel Josiah Wedgwood.

First Commissioner of Works, Mr. F. W. Jowett.

The last two offices did not confer Cabinet rank in the last Government, but it is probable that they will in the present one. As Mr. MacDonald, besides the Premiership, holds two other

Continued at Foot of Next Column

THE PREMIER'S MESSAGE TO OUR READERS

Our Lobby correspondent, who was among the first to greet the Labour Leader as "Mr. Prime Minister," received from him the following message to DAILY HERALD readers:—

"I wish to send my very great thanks to the readers of the 'Daily Herald,' and to say that the best way they can show their appreciation of what has happened is to continue to support the paper with greater enthusiasm than ever."

Continued from Previous Column

Cabinet appointments, the total number of Cabinet Ministers would not be increased, if, as probable, Colonel Wedgwood and Mr. Jowett were included.

The exchange of seals will take place at noon to-day.

YET TO BE FILLED

The appointments now announced leave yet to be filled those Ministries which do not confer Cabinet rank.

These comprised in the last Government the offices of Attorney- and Solicitor-General, Minister of Pensions, Financial Secretary to the Treasury, Parliamentary Secretary to the Treasury, Junior Lords of the Treasury (four), Paymaster-General, Civil Lord of the Admiralty, six Under-Secretaries (Air, Colonial, Foreign, Home, India, and War), 11 Under-Secretaries (Admiralty, Agriculture, Board of Trade, Education, Health, Labour, Transport, Pensions, Mines, Overseas Trade, and War), and the Lord Advocate, Solicitor-General, and Under-Secretary for Health for Scotland.

TWO AUDIENCES

It was just after noon yesterday that Mr. MacDonald had an audience of the King at Buckingham Palace.

First, he had to be sworn in as a member of the Privy Council. This was a necessary preliminary to taking office. The other Privy Councillors present were Lord Salisbury, Sir John Simon, Mr. Rawlinson, K.C., Mr. Arthur Henderson, Mr. J. R. Clynes, and Mr. J. H. Thomas.

The King detained Mr. MacDonald for an hour's conversation, but could

Continued on Page Five, Col. Four

WHY CABINET IS LARGE ONE

Plans for Working on Business-like Lines

MEETING TO-DAY

The first meeting of the new Cabinet will be held at 10, Downing-street, at 4 p.m. to-day (writes our Lobby Correspondent).

The great, and, I believe, unprecedented promptitude with which the new Cabinet has been announced and is taking over the Administration has created a very favourable impression.

The filling up of the Under-Secretaryships is, I am able to state, almost completed, and a full announcement may be expected in a day or two. I believe it will be found that the new Minister of Mines is Mr. Shinwell.

The Cabinet will be a large one. The reason for this it that a great deal of the work will be done by Committees of Ministers.

These committees will thresh out the questions referred to them and report their conclusions to the full Cabinet, the functions of which will be to supervise and make the final decisions. Thus the country will have for the first time a Government organised on business lines, and able to perform the nation's business with thoroughness.

Mr. MacDonald has adopted the time-tested plan of placing at the head of a department, not an expert in the affairs of that department, but a man who can be trusted to bring common sense and political judgment to bear upon it.

The experts to whom some of the "guessers," proceeding upon a contrary principle, had assigned departments are in the Cabinet, and their special knowledge will be available on the Committees and in the general Cabinet councils.

"I SHALL LIKE IT"

Miss MacDonald's Verdict on No. 10

At the invitation of Mrs. Baldwin, Miss MacDonald, still a girl at college, paid a visit of inspection to No. 10, Downing-street yesterday.

She was conducted through the many chambers of the official residence of Britain's Prime Ministers by an attendant, who gave her points of their history and development. She saw where the Cabinet had met only a few minutes before her own arrival.

At the conclusion of this minute inspection she was persuaded to stand on the doorstep, and a curious crowd watched with interest while she was being photographed.

"How do you like your new home?" said a pressman.

"It's awfully complicated," was the unexpected reply, "but I think I shall like it."

RAIL STRIKE LEADERS PROPOSE PARLEY

But Managers Insist on Acceptance of Wages Board's Award

"DISCUSS DIFFERENCES"

—Loco Union's Offer

Correspondence passed yesterday between the railway managers and the Associated Society, whose members are on strike. The managers, while prepared to meet the men's leaders, repeated their insistence on acceptance of the Wages Board's award.

The Executive of the Associated Society replied by reiterating its willingness to meet the managers to discuss the adjustment of differences.

"N.U.R. men in all parts of the country are joining us," said an A.S.L.E. and F. official last night. Other statements by union officials, and reports from strike areas, are printed on Page Three.

INDUSTRY SLOWS DOWN

There was an important development in the situation yesterday. Early in the day it was announced that the railway managers were meeting to consider a letter from the Executive of the Associated Society.

"I am requested by the Executive Committee," Mr. Bromley wrote, "to inform the general managers that my Committee is prepared at any time to meet the General Managers for a conference to endeavour to adjust existing difficulties."

MANAGERS' REPLY

The managers, in their reply, declared that

Proposals unanimously endorsed by the General Council of the Trades Union Congress are still open for acceptance by your Society. They represent the full extent to which the companies are prepared to go.

"The public statement recently made by you indicates that your society is still opposed to the adoption of the decision of the National Wages Board, and so long as that position continues it is difficult to see that any advantage is to be gained by holding a meeting such as you suggest.

"If, having regard to what has been said above, your Executive Committee thinks an interview desirable, the general managers are prepared to arrange for one with you."

This was considered by the Executive of the Associated Society last night, when it was decided to intimate again to the managers willingness to meet them and request them to arrange a meeting with the Executive "with a view to the adjustment of existing differences."

"READY TO MEET YOU"

The loco. men's reply stated:—

"We desire to say that the efforts of the General Council of the Trades Union Congress were highly appreciated, but it must be understood that any action taken by them was solely on their own initiative as an intermediary body.

"We regret that apparently the General Managers refuse to set aside the findings of the National Wages Board.

"We would again point out that such findings were rejected by our members by a ballot vote, and further, the locomotive men of Great Britain have demonstrated by direct action their opposition to such findings.

"We again express our willingness to meet the general managers with the object of securing the adjustment of existing differences, and would request them to arrange a meeting with this Executive Committee at their convenience."

"STRONG GESTURE"

Mr. Moore, assistant secretary to the Society, described the approach to the companies as the gesture of a strong man. "Our Executive felt, and feels, strongly," he said, "that the parties should not sit each on its own fence without any effort to end the dispute."

Mr Bromley said last night that he saw little in the managers' letter beyond an attempt to place the Society in a false position.

It was untrue that the General Council of the Trades Union Congress assented to or endorsed any proposals from the managers.

[Note.—The statement to the contrary was issued by the railway companies on Sunday, but appeared to be an agreed report.]

Some light is thrown on the difficulty which caused the breakdown of the negotiations conducted last Saturday by the Trades Union Congress General Council, in a circular issued by Mr. John Turner (a member of the Council) to the members of the Shop Assistants' Union.

Mr. Turner points out that the Associated Society felt that the managers' demand that the strike notices should be withdrawn was intended to prejudice the men's position, "since no guarantee that the negotiations would bring any relief accompanied that request.

"Had the same assurance with respect to the serious hardships being redressed been given, as was the case with respect to the feared dismissals, some last-minute settlement might possibly have been secured."

LENIN DIES SUDDENLY

POIGNANT SCENE IN THE SOVIET

A LONG SILENCE

MOSCOW MOURNS GREAT LEADER

Nicolai Lenin (Vladimir Ilyitch Oulianoff) died at 6.50 on Monday evening at Gorky, in the hills near Moscow.

He had seemed to be recovering from his long illness—the aftermath of his attempted assassination in 1918; but suddenly on Monday afternoon he became worse. Paralysis of the respiratory organs set in. At 5.30 breathing became difficult. He lost consciousness, and died at 6.50.

The All-Russian Soviet Congress was in session yesterday morning at the Bolshoi Theatre in Moscow, when Kalenin—the President of the Republic—tears streaming down his face—told the news. The great assembly rose and stood for five minutes in silence, very many of them weeping. And from the theatre word spread through Moscow—already draped in black in honour of the heroes of 1905.

To-day the body will be brought to Moscow, and will lie in state in the hall of the great Trade Union Palace on the banks of the Moskava.

And on Saturday Lenin will be buried, by the side of his friend Sverdlov, in the holy place of Revolutionary Russia—in the Red Square of Moscow, under the great wall of the Kremlin, among the nameless workers who fell in the Revolution of 1917.

[A biographical sketch on Lenin appears on Page Five.]

How to avoid 'flu

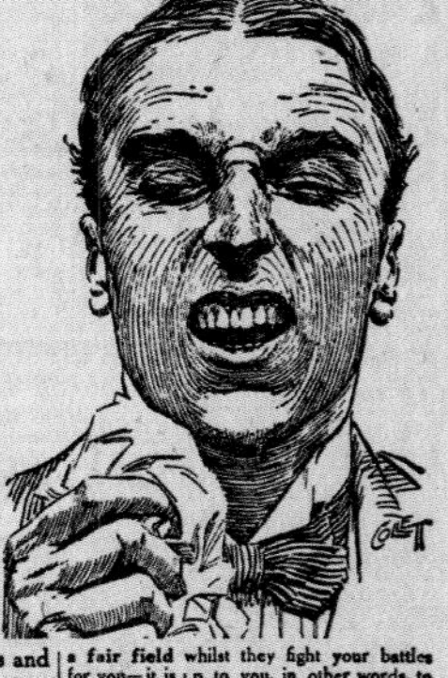

Prevention is better than cure, and, in view of the fact that influenza is claiming hundreds of fresh victims every week, it is wise to see how the germs of influenza work and how we can beat them at their own game.

The way disease germ work is as follows: They obtain a lodgment in recesses of your nose, mouth, throat, and even stomach or intestines, where they generate their virus and distribute it throughout the system by the body's common carrier, the blood.

If you allow it!

Nature has evolved an efficient system of defence against these germs. Myriads of tiny corpuscles which travel with your blood stream are the natural defenders of the central citadel—the nervous system—of your health. They are of two kinds, red and white. The red ones energise your body to resist infection generally; the white ones raid these disease germs and (whisper it!) devour them bodily.

It rests with you to give these corpuscles a fair field whilst they fight your battles for you—it is up to you, in other words, to "keep the ring."

The area of operations is your blood, and if the blood be pure and virile, there is not a germ in all bacteriology that has the power to impair your energy, efficiency, and general well-being.

The Kruschen habit is your first line of defence against disease germs: because it enables Nature to maintain a rich supply of pure and virile blood.

Kruschen Salts is a *natural* aperient and diuretic tonic—not a medicine, but an "aid to Nature" in eliminating from the system waste material which poisons and debilitates the blood. The bowel, liver, kidney, lungs, and skin—the body organs of elimination—all work better and more regularly under the daily reminder of the Kruschen habit, and with these organs working well and regularly, the purity and virility of the blood is ensured.

Your first line of defence

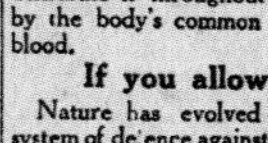

Tasteless in Tea

Put as much in your breakfast cup as will lie on a sixpence. It's the little daily dose that does it.

Kruschen Salts

Good Health for a Farthing a Day

Take as much Kruschen Salts as will lie on a sixpence every morning in your breakfast cup of tea. This is your first safeguard against epidemics, etc., such as influenza—and, too, the indispensable condition precedent to their successful treatment.

Economy—A bottle of Kruschen Salts costs 1s. 9d., and lasts three months. Health and spirits for less than a farthing a day. Get a bottle at your chemist's to-day, and start to-morrow.

JANUARY

22 MONDAY

23 TUESDAY

24 WEDNESDAY

25 THURSDAY   First Quarter

26 FRIDAY   *Holiday, Australia (Australia Day)*

27 SATURDAY

28 SUNDAY

Daily Herald, Wednesday, 23 January 1924: Britain's first Labour government is formed.

JANUARY ~ FEBRUARY

29 MONDAY

30 TUESDAY

31 WEDNESDAY

1 THURSDAY

2 FRIDAY   Full Moon

3 SATURDAY

4 SUNDAY

Daily Mirror, Monday, 31 January 1972: Bloody Sunday in Londonderry.

Daily Mirror

BRITAIN'S BIGGEST DAILY SALE

Monday, January 31, 1972 • No. 21,167

ULSTER'S BLOODY SUNDAY

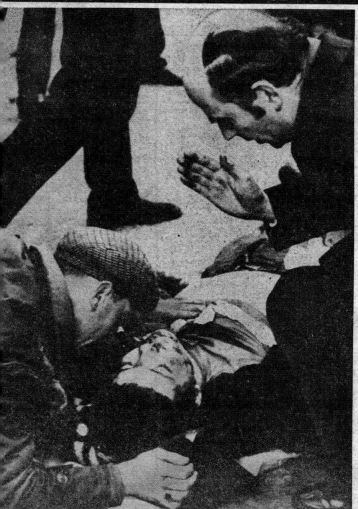

LAST RITES

Kneeling in the road, a priest gives the last rites to a dying demonstrator . . . Picture by Stanley Matchett. More of his dramatic pictures—See Centre Pages.

From JOE GORROD in Londonderry

THIRTEEN men were killed yesterday as Army paratroopers broke up a banned Civil Rights march in Londonderry.

Another twelve people—including two women and a child—were wounded by bullets when the Paras stormed into the Catholic Bogside area.

The soldiers claimed last night that they opened fire when they came under sniper attack. They said they were arresting about fifty demonstrators who had been hurling stones at troops behind barricades.

Five soldiers were hurt in the fierce battle—three of them hit by stones and two burned by acid bombs.

March

Eighteen demonstrators were taken to hospital with injuries that were not caused by bullets.

The marchers who died were aged between sixteen and forty.

Last night shocked Civil Rights leaders were calling the incident a massacre.

Bernadette Devlin, the Mid-Ulster MP who took part in the anti-internment march, said: "It was mass murder by the Army.

"This was our Sharpe-

13 die.. Army accused of 'massacre'

ville, and we shall never forget it."

Miss Devlin was referring to the killing of sixty-seven Africans by South African police in 1960.

She claimed: "The troops shot up a peaceful meeting. Then they let loose with bloodthirsty gusto at anything that strayed into their sights.

"Let nobody say that they fired in retaliation."

Mr. John Hume, Londonderry's MP at Stormont, declared: "It was cold-blooded mass murder—another bloody Sunday."

And Mr. Ivan Cooper, MP for Mid-Derry, said: "The soldiers showed no mercy. I was shot at while waving a white flag. People

were falling all over the street."

There were immediate threats of revenge from the official IRA in Dublin, and the Provisional IRA in Londonderry.

A spokesman for the provisionals claimed: "At no time did any of our units open fire on the Army prior to the Army opening fire."

The shooting broke out as 12,000 demonstrators who had marched through the Bogside tried to pass barricades put up to stop them getting into the city centre.

Some of the marchers fought a forty-five-minute battle with troops before men of the 1st Battalion of the Parachute Regiment burst through the barricades and charged into the crowd to make arrests.

Bodies

Minutes afterwards the first shots rang out.

The bodies of two men, claimed by the Army to have been firing at them, were recovered by troops.

A public inquiry into the shooting was demanded last night by Cardinal William Conway, Primate of All Ireland.

He said:

"I have received a first-hand account from a priest who was present at the scene, and what I have heard is really shocking.

"An impartial and independent public inquiry is immediately called for, and I have telegraphed the British Prime Minister to this effect."

'SOLDIERS DIDN'T FIRE FIRST SHOT'

THE Army's Ulster chief claimed last night that his men did not "go in shooting" against yesterday's marchers in Londonderry.

"They did not fire until they were fired upon," said Major General Robert Ford, commander of land forces in the province.

He claimed that the dead "might not have been killed by our soldiers."

General Ford said in a

BBC TV interview that the paratroops' aim was to arrest hooligans who had been attacking them for two hours.

As the soldiers went in, acid bombs were dropped from a block of flats and two of them were injured — one seriously.

At the same time gun-

■ Continued on Page Two

Fans on a roof at London Airport wave goodbye to the Beatles yesterday.

3d.   Saturday, February 8, 1964   ◆   No. 18,704

YEAH! YEAH! U.S.A

That old Beatlemania hits New York . . . a screaming girl tries to get nearer the Beatles.

Paul, Ringo, George and John answer questions at the Press con...

FATHER FLIES TO GET IRENE

PRINCESS Irene of Holland, whose romance has started a constitutional crisis, is going home today.

It was announced last night that her father, Prince Bernhard, would fly to Spain to pick her up.

And in Madrid, the Spanish capital, Irene's secretary stated early to-day that her engagement to a Spanish nobleman will be announced by "the Dutch Royal House in Holland."

Marry

But there were strong rumours in The Hague, the Dutch capital, last night that 24-year-old Irene will give up her rights of succession to the throne and marry the man she loves.

'Engagement news soon'

Irene—who recently became a Roman Catholic—is second in line to the Dutch Throne after her sister Beatrix.

Yesterday Prince Bernhard flew his own plane to Austria and took Beatrix and her younger sister, Princess Margriet, home to Holland. They had been on holiday, watching the winter Olympics.

Their arrival in The Hague strengthened reports that the Dutch Royal family is gathering for an important meeting when Irene arrives today.

The announcement that Irene would be returning home today said that she had been spending several days in a "house of retreat" in Spain.

A second Government statement denied rumours that Queen Juliana might abdicate because of differences with the Cabinet over Irene's romance.

The Dutch Cabinet met again last night. Later Prime Minister Victor Marijnen, asked to comment on the "engagement" statement in Madrid, said: "We will know more when the Princess is back here."

From BARRIE HARDING
New York, Friday

FIVE thousand screaming, chanting teenagers—most of them playing truant from school—gave the Beatles a fantastic welcome here today.

More than 100 extra police were on duty to control the crowd as the group's jet landed at the John F. Kennedy Airport.

'Mad'

Pandemonium broke out among the stamping, banner-waving fans as the Beatles—John Lennon, Paul McCartney, George Harrison and Ringo Starr—stepped from the plane.

One policeman who has worked at the airport for ten years said : " I think

---

5,000 scream 'welcome' to the Beatles

the world has gone mad."

And a veteran airport employee said : "I see it—but I don't believe it."

As the Beatles waved and clowned, teenagers at the front of the crowd on the airport roof struggled to keep from falling to the tarmac, 20ft. below.

Then, when the group had left the plane, thousands of their screaming fans rushed to the balcony above the Customs Hall to watch them pass through.

Girls between fourteen and twenty-two pressed their noses against the big windows, waiting for the Beatles to pass by.

There were screams and shouts as their guitars appeared on a luggage trolley.

There were fresh squeals as the Beatles finally appeared, surrounded by a "bodyguard" of New York policemen.

Fans waved huge posters. There was a huge banner which proclaimed "Welcome to Beatlesville, U.S.A."

One of the fans had travelled 1,500 miles from Arkansas to see the group arrive—and many more had travelled up to 300 miles.

Airport officials said the

---

crowd rivalled ... since General M... returned from Ko...

The airport Pre... ence which follo... Beatles' arrival w...

Hundreds of ... and photographe... seven TV camera... room bursting at ...

Mone

Part of the que... answer session be... porters and Bea... like this :

"Will you sir ... thing ?"

John Lennon : ... "Can you sing ? ... "Not without a ... "How much ... you expect to ma... USA?"

George Ha... "About half a cro... "Are you goin... haircuts ?" Lennon : "We ... yesterday."

They were al... what they thoug... anti-Beatle cam...

Continued ...
Back Pa...

FEBRUARY

---

5 MONDAY

---

6 TUESDAY   *Holiday, New Zealand (Waitangi Day)*

---

7 WEDNESDAY

---

8 THURSDAY

---

9 FRIDAY

---

10 SATURDAY   Last Quarter

---

11 SUNDAY

Daily Mirror, Saturday, 8 February 1964: the Beatles go to America.

FEBRUARY

12 MONDAY   *Holiday, USA (Lincoln's birthday)*

---

13 TUESDAY

---

14 WEDNESDAY   *St Valentine's Day*

---

15 THURSDAY

---

16 FRIDAY

---

17 SATURDAY   New Moon

---

18 SUNDAY   *Chinese New Year*

Daily Mirror, Monday, 15 February 1971: the decimalization of Britain's currency.

DAILY Mirror

(6d.) Monday, February 15, 1971 · No. 20,876

ALL CHANGE!

Good Morning! It's D-Day

...ATERHOUSE
...already ...n driven ...ty . .
— Page 6

...EITH WAITE
...s seen ...ll ...ore
— Page 5

...OUR MIRROR

The Daily Mirror is today priced at 2½ ...w pence, which is the ...act equivalent of the ... you have been paying. ...But you can still buy ...ur Mirror—Britain's ...ggest-selling ...wspaper—with a ...xpenny piece which is ...maining in circulation.

GOING TO BE ... REAT WEEK IN ... MIRROR ...UR BEST BUY ...NY CURRENCY

BRITISH RAIL went decimal yesterday. One of the first customers at Brighton, Sussex, was Jenny Farley, 16. She's still at school, and knows all about the new money. There are obviously no problems for Jenny.

KEEP your cool. Take your time. And don't let them rush you. That is our advice on this Happy (we hope) D-Day.

Three thousand readers have already had their decimal problems solved by the Mirror Decimal Watchdogs—the best and most active service of its kind in Britain.

Now D-Day has arrived. So here is how to get through this historic Monday as painlessly as possible!

To start with, it's all much easier than most people imagine.

1—TAKE plenty of small change out with you this morning.

Soon you'll be paying with decimal bronze coins—½p, 1p, 2p. But as you haven't got any yet, when you go into decimal shops you will have to pay in £sd amounts made up to the nearest sixpence above the price.

That's because sixpence is the lowest £sd sum with **EXACT** decimal value—2½p. If you don't pay in 6d units, you'll be diddling yourself because the shopkeeper won't be able to give you the correct change.

2—TAKE your Mirror Shoppers' guide, which is printed today on Page 5, if you want to compare the old £sd prices with the new decimal ones.

But remember that you cannot use this table to choose whether you pay in £sd or the £p prices. Think—and pay—**DECIMAL**.

Remember also that in decimal shops where you buy

several items, like the local newsagents for instance, the shopkeeper must total up each of the items separately in decimals—then charge you the decimal total.

He can't just convert the £sd total to decimals.

3—TAKE your time. If you think a mistake has been made, don't worry about holding up the queue. Ask the cashier immediately. But try not to lose your patience.

Fair

Most shopkeepers, who have spent a lot of time and money going decimal, intend to play fair—but it's likely to be a rather fraught start to the week for them too.

4—IF you get really confused and decide it's all too much for you, pick up the nearest telephone and ring the Mirror's Decimal Watchdogs.

We're here to help you.

DIAL (01) 822 3962 if you live in these areas: London, Birmingham, Bristol, Cambridge, Cardiff, Leicester, Nottingham, Oxford, Plymouth, Southampton, Wolverhampton.

DIAL (061) 829 2225 if you live in these areas: Manchester, Belfast, Carlisle, Chester, Hull, Leeds, Liverpool, Middlesborough, Newcastle, North Wales, Preston, Sheffield.

DIAL (041) 248 7000 if you live in these areas: Glasgow, Aberdeen, Dundee, Edinburgh.

And good luck!

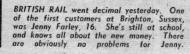

NEW PENNY JENNY

THE WICKED DECEIT THAT JAILED THE BRIDGEWATER FOUR BY PAUL FOOT, THE JOURNALIST WHO DID MOST TO FREE THEM

The Observer

THE COLOUR OF BRITAIN AFTER LABOUR'S VICTORY
SEE THE TIDDLER

SUNDAY 23 FEBRUARY 1997 ESTABLISHED 1791 £1

Scientists clone adult sheep

Triumph for UK raises alarm over human use

by Robin McKie
Science Editor

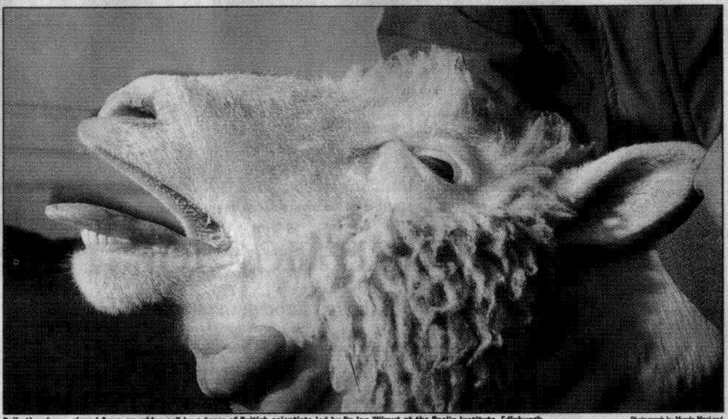

Dolly the sheep, cloned from an udder cell by a team of British scientists led by Dr Ian Wilmut at the Roslin Institute, Edinburgh. Photograph by Murdo MacLeod

SCIENTISTS have created the first clone of an adult animal. They have taken a cell from a sheep's udder and turned it into a lamb.

The development is a landmark in biological research — and a triumph for UK science, one that should lead to breakthroughs in work on ageing, genetics and medicines.

But cloning is also likely to cause alarm. The technique could be used on humans, drawing parallels with Huxley's *Brave New World* and the film *The Boys from Brazil*, in which clones of Hitler are made.

Human cloning, although now close to reality, would be illegal under the laws governing fertilisation research. No responsible biologist would support such work, say scientists.

The crucial cloning experiment took place at the Roslin Institute, near Edinburgh. A team led by Dr Ian Wilmut took a single cell — from the udder of an adult sheep — and turned it into a viable embryo, which was implanted in a surrogate mother. A few weeks ago that sheep gave birth to a lamb, Dolly, due to be introduced to the public for the first time on Wednesday. Dolly is genetically identical to the sheep from which the cell was taken.

Until now scientists have achieved only limited results in cloning animals, though the procedure is common in plant breeding. In one case tadpole cells were used to clone frogs. This is the first time a viable offspring has been grown from an adult animal's cell, however.

This success follows years of pioneering work at Roslin. Last year the team made news worldwide when it cloned sheep embryos. The researchers took an egg from a sheep and removed the nucleus containing its genetic material. Then they took a cell from an immature embryo from a different sheep and removed its nucleus. This was then used to replace the nucleus removed from the egg of the first sheep.

Out of 250 attempts, two embryos developed into lambs: Morag and Megan, clones of the original embryo. But early embryo cells are easier to clone than adult ones because they have not differentiated into muscle, heart or brain cells.

The new breakthrough was achieved by Dr Wilmut who created chemical baths in which adult cells — in this case from a sheep's mammary gland — could be soaked. In this way, their nuclei were turned into a quiescent state. The division of each nucleus's genetic material was slowed down to a rate acceptable to the egg cells into which they were placed.

As a result, the team — whose work will feature in a forthcoming edition of Carlton TV's *Network First* — was able to remove the mammary gland cell's nucleus, treat it and then place into a different sheep's egg cell. This embryo remained viable, and developed into Dolly.

The breakthrough has enormous importance, much of it immediate. For example, it is now possible to genetically engineer sheep so they make human medicines, such as blood clotting factors, in their milk — though the procedure is awkward. By cloning such an animal it will now be possible to create flocks of medicine-making sheep.

And by using an old animal's genes to make an embryo, scientists will gain new insights into ageing. The accumulation of tiny genetic errors is thought to produce changes to the body as an animal grows old. Now scientists can study those processes in detail.

However, it is the prospect of cloning people, creating armies of dictators, that will attract most attention. The Roslin technique could, theoretically, be used on humans. A sheep is a complex mammal, after all, so cloning one raises concerns. Whether anyone would wish to clone a human is a different matter.

LET THEM EAT LESS, PRISONS CHIEF WAS TOLD

Mrs Howard's own recipe for prison reform

by David Leigh

SANDRA PAUL, the former model and wife of Home Secretary Michael Howard, tried to cut the quality of the food served to Britain's 50,000 prisoners.

She also queried recommended prison hygiene and laundry standards, former prisons director Derek Lewis says he was told, in an explosive television interview to be shown tomorrow.

The four-times-married Ms Paul thought a proposed code of prison standards submitted to her husband was 'too generous', Mr Lewis has told Granada TV's *World in Action*.

The Home Office last year had to pay more than £215,000 compensation to Mr Lewis to settle a wrongful dismissal suit he brought for being sacked by Mr Howard after a row over who was responsible for the prison system's failings.

Mr Lewis says: 'I was extremely surprised to be asked to take into account and to incorporate a number of concerns Mrs Howard apparently had about the code of standards.'

He adds that David Cameron, Mr Howard's political adviser, told him it was Mrs Howard's opinion, relayed via the Home Secretary, 'that the code's requirement to provide a balanced and nutritious diet was somehow too generous for prisoners'.

He made some of the changes she requested, to dilute laundry and hygiene standards, but refused to cut the nutrition code. 'These suggestions I considered were unacceptable.'

Mr Lewis says the food standards were 'essential to providing decent and humane conditions'. The code finally sent to prisons in April 1994 said: 'Meals should be varied, nutritious and prepared to an approved standard. The menu for each meal should be varied and reflect modern eating habits.'

Prisoners were to be allowed showers or baths no more than three times a week; their sheets were to be washed weekly; but their blankets only monthly.

Mr Lewis tells *World in Action* that Mr Howard never wanted a code of standards in the first place: 'He was very concerned that this would be seen simply as a charter for prisoners and would provoke a hostile public reaction.'

Mr Lewis says he was taken aside in early 1994 by an uncomfortable Mr Cameron. The Old Etonian political adviser showed him a 'his and hers' list. Mr Howard wanted some changes, while Mrs Howard proposed a list of 'housekeeping' suggestions of her own to toughen up the code of standards.

'It was a surprising source for it to have come from,' he says.

Mr Howard and Mr Lewis had angry altercations about the code in February 1994, with the Home Secretary continuing to fear he would be open to tabloid criticism for 'pampering' convicts.

The final showdown with the £165,000-a-year prisons director came in 1995. After an escape of inmates from Parkhurst, Mr Howard sacked Mr Lewis in an attempt to make him take the blame for shortcomings in the prisons service.

Mr Howard is currently under investigation by the Parliamentary Standards Commissioner, Sir Gordon Downey. The owner of Harrods, Mohammed al-Fayed, alleges that when he was Trade Minister Mr Howard was involved in a decision to order a DTI inquiry into Mr Fayed's background. He claims Mr Howard's cousin, Harry Landy, brought pressure on the Minister to act against the Harrods owner. Mr Landy had previously been connected with Mr Fayed's business rival, Tiny Rowland.

Sir Gordon is inquiring into Mr Howard's position as part of his investigation into the 'sleaze' disclosures about former Minister Neil Hamilton and other Tory MPs.

Mr Cameron, Conservative prospective candidate for Stafford at the forthcoming general election, said last week he was not prepared to deny Mr Lewis's disclosures. 'I don't want to say anything on the record at all.'

Mr Howard, who was yesterday in his Folkestone constituency, issued a limited denial, saying it was untrue there was 'a list' of suggestions from his wife. Last night solicitor John Turnbull from Linklaters & Paines called the Observer on Mrs Howard's behalf, denying Mr Lewis's allegations. He said: 'She has never had any discussions with her husband or anyone else about the nutritional standards in the code.'

WHAT THE PRISONERS GET: 'TOO GENEROUS,' SAYS SANDRA

This is the everyday diet in a mainstream British prison, according to Nick Flynn, deputy director of the Prison Reform Trust. It is produced under the 1994 Code of Standards which the prisons' director was told Sandra Howard found 'too generous'. Flynn says, 'On balance, a prisoner's diet is less nutritious than the average out in the community.'

LOW-GRADE MEAT PIE, PROCESSED
PEAS AND CHIPS
MORE CHIPS
('A prisoner with a belly-full of starchy food is less of a control problem')
STEAMED SPONGE PUDDING
TEA

WHAT THE HOME SECRETARY GETS: 'WONDERFUL,' SAYS SANDRA

In 1994, as Lewis reacted in dismay to her plan for cutting prison diets, the Sixties model was confiding to Healthy Eating magazine that the Home Secretary was 'wonderful to cook for'. She was later quoted as having jibbed at giving details: 'Michael is cutting back on food in prisons at the moment, you see.' But she eventually revealed his favourite menu.

OYSTERS
CARROT AND ORANGE SOUP
('Michael finds soup comforting')
DUCK A L'ORANGE
CREME BRULEE
('When he's 12st 7lb he gives up pudding')
RED WINE

Taxman outwitted over £22m debt

by Michael Gillard, David Connett and Jonathan Calvert

A FORMER City stockbroker cheated the Inland Revenue out of £22 million in unpaid taxes through a series of remarkable deals in which he agreed to inform on his clients and testify against corrupt tax investigator Michael Allcock.

The Revenue agreed that Jonathan Bekhor only need pay a fraction of what he owed. But much of the promised information was later dismissed as unreliable and malicious. He has only paid £10,000 to the Revenue. The prosecution did not call him as a witness against Allcock after he gave contradictory statements.

As Allcock began his five-year sentence last week, Bekhor was in California, immune from prosecution. The *Observer* has learnt that, although branded a liar by senior tax officials, the Revenue continued to deal with Bekhor seeking names and cash.

To save himself, Bekhor falsely implicated Deputy Prime Minister Michael Heseltine.

The Revenue agreed to accept £1.25m — later halved to £650,000 — in settlement of Bekhor's £22m debt. Payments stopped after a cheque bounced in 1995.

Bekhor agreed to testify against Allcock, who investigated his affairs for four years from 1988. Described by Allcock as 'a very shrewd operator', Bekhor was the focus of the Revenue's 'Stock Exchange Project' which targeted share dealing profits hidden in offshore tax havens.

As his firm, AJ Bekhor, lurched towards bankruptcy in 1989, Bekhor, 51 next week, decided to co-operate. He handed over confidential details on 50,000 clients and provided Allcock with a 'top 20 list' and promised documents on six 'prominent' names, one of whom was Mr Heseltine. Bekhor claimed he was linked to a Swiss-based share dealing syndicate. No evidence was produced and the Revenue decided an investigation was unjustified.

Mr Heseltine denies knowing or having any business links to Bekhor or the individuals he named.

Talks on a new deal for names and cash were still going on when Allcock was suspended in September 1992. In 1993, the Revenue allowed Bekhor to cancel his personal bankruptcy in return for the reduced £650,000 payment. Soon after Bekhor agreed to testify against Allcock. But last year Bekhor changed his story to detectives, undermining his value as a witness.

Tax secrets of the stars, page 8

REDFORD AND ME
BY JAMES LASDUN. IN THE REVIEW

'If a man fancies Felicity Kendal, he is sexually defunct'
BY LYNN BARBER

IN LIFE

LONDON FASHION WEEK
McQueen

The men behind him

ALSO IN LIFE

Full index on page 2

08>
9 770029 771120
★★★★ G 10714

FEBRUARY

---

19 MONDAY   *Holiday, USA (Presidents' Day)*

---

20 TUESDAY   *Shrove Tuesday*

---

21 WEDNESDAY   *Ash Wednesday*

---

22 THURSDAY

---

23 FRIDAY

---

24 SATURDAY   First Quarter

---

25 SUNDAY

The Observer, Sunday, 23 February 1997: scientists create Dolly the sheep, the first animal clone.

FEBRUARY ~ MARCH

26 MONDAY

27 TUESDAY

28 WEDNESDAY

1 THURSDAY   *St David's Day*

2 FRIDAY

3 SATURDAY   Full Moon

4 SUNDAY

Daily Mail, Thursday, 29 February 1996: the announcement of the divorce of the Prince and Princess of Wales.

NIGEL DEMPSTER	THE MONEY	THE CHILDREN	PAUL JOHNSON
Why Charles will never marry Camilla PAGE 4	**Why Diana insists on £15 million** PAGE 6	**How Wills and Harry took the news** PAGE 7	**What hope is there for marriage now?** PAGE 8

DIVORCE

Exclusive: The secret teatime meeting that sealed Diana's fate

By
RICHARD
KAY

AFTER weeks of relentless Royal pressure, the Princess of Wales finally agreed last night to the divorce she did not want.

At secret teatime talks with Prince Charles, Diana even agreed to give up the title of Her Royal Highness.

She will be known simply as Diana, Princess of Wales.

An announcement after the 45-minute meeting at St James's Palace said Diana would be involved 'in all decisions relating to the children' and would continue to live at Kensington Palace.

Now lawyers on both sides will begin the tough negotiations towards a financial settlement, expected to be worth at least £15million to the princess. She has indicated she will not settle for less.

News of the deal was clouded by yet more wrangling between the two camps. Diana was accused of breaking a secrecy agreement and announcing details which had not yet been agreed, charges she strongly denied.

Her aides said they made the announcement only after details leaked from elsewhere.

Divorce — which could now be only weeks away — became inevitable at Christmas when the Queen wrote to both Charles and Diana urging them to make their separation final.

Charles agreed at once, but Diana made it clear that she would reach a decision in her own time. Since then she has been under continual pressure to do so quickly. Her meeting with Charles followed an exchange of personal letters over the weekend. The prince

Diana: 'I have given them everything they want'

Turn to Page 4, Col. 1

Charles: After visiting a Hindu temple yesterday

MAIL ON SUNDAY 2 TODAY

MARCH 8, 1987

The Mail

ON SUNDAY

40p

YOU The finest magazine

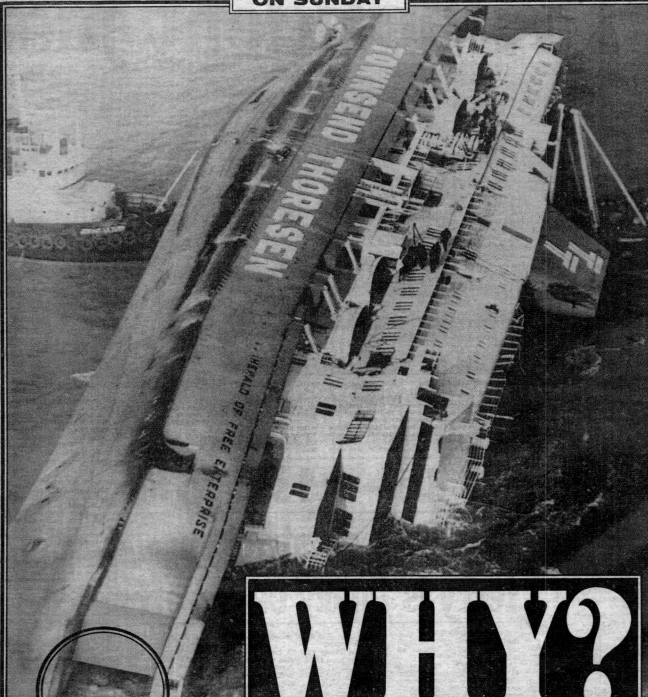

WHY?
Open door clue to ferry disaster

FULL STORY: Pages 2, 3, 4, 5, 6 and 7

MARCH

5 MONDAY

6 TUESDAY

7 WEDNESDAY

8 THURSDAY

9 FRIDAY

10 SATURDAY

11 SUNDAY

The Mail on Sunday, 8 March 1987: the *Herald of Free Enterprise* capsizes at Zeebrugge.

MARCH

---

12 MONDAY
Commonwealth Day
Last Quarter

---

13 TUESDAY

---

14 WEDNESDAY

---

15 THURSDAY

---

16 FRIDAY

---

17 SATURDAY

---

18 SUNDAY
Mothering Sunday, UK

Daily Express: Saturday, 12 March 1938: Germany invades Austria.

DAILY EXPRESS, Saturday, March 12, 1938

Daily Express

WORLD'S LARGEST DAILY SALE

No. 11,798 Saturday, March 12, 1938 One Penny

Schuschnigg Resigns: 'I Yield To Force'

GERMANS MARCH INTO AUSTRIA

Britain Makes Protest "In Strongest Terms"

Austrian Nazis' Call To Hitler: 'Send Troops To Avoid Shedding Blood'

FALLEN IDOL

HITLER forced Dr. von Schuschnigg to resign the Chancellorship of Austria last night. The Austrian Nazis sent an S O S to Berlin for armed assistance "to avoid bloodshed." At 11.15 p.m., for the first time since the great war, German troops marched across the Austrian frontier.

Two regiments of German artillery occupied the upper Austrian capital of Linz without a shot being fired. German infantry marched on Salzburg from the mountains of Bavaria.

As soon as the news of Dr. Schuschnigg's resignation was confirmed the French and British Ambassadors in Berlin made a joint démarche to the German Government. The British protest appears in Column 1.

With an ultimatum from the German Chancellor on his desk, an ultimatum expiring at six o'clock, Chancellor Schuschnigg's four years' battle for Austria's independence collapsed with drastic suddenness. Dr. Artur Seyss Inquart, thirty-five-year-old lawyer, pro-German Minister for Public Security in Schuschnigg's Cabinet, is expected to be the new Austrian Chancellor.

Nazis have taken over command of the eight provincial Governments. Orders were broadcast first by Schuschnigg himself, then by Dr. Seyss-Inquart, ordering no resistance to German invasion.

It was at 6.30 p.m. that Dr. Schuschnigg announced that the nation-wide plebiscite announced for

► PAGE TWO, COL. ONE

BRITISH PROTEST

'Bound To Produce Grave Reactions'

Here is the text of the communique issued at the Foreign Office late last night:—

"On instructions from his Majesty's Government, the British Ambassador in Berlin, in reference to the contents of the second German ultimatum, registered a protest in the strongest possible terms against such a use of coercion backed by force against an independent State in order to create a situation incompatible with its national independence.

"Such action, it was pointed out, is bound to produce the gravest reactions of which it is impossible to foretell the issue."

The French Ambassador in Berlin made a similar protest.

CABINET TO MEET THIS MORNING

MR. CHAMBERLAIN has called a Cabinet meeting at Downing-street this morning.

The decision was taken after consultation with Lord Halifax, Foreign Secretary, and other Cabinet Ministers, who maintained close contact with Downing-street all last night.

All Ministers were in London last night, having been warned earlier in the day to stand by and fulfil no out-of-town engagements at the week-end.

Here, staring from a plebiscite-appeal poster in Vienna, is Schuschnigg.—Picture wired yesterday from Austria.

60,000 German Troops Mass On Frontier

From ERNEST POPE
Daily Express Correspondent
MUNICH, Friday.

TEN THOUSAND German troops are massed tonight in Kiefersfelden and Rosenheim, towns on the Austrian frontier. Another 50,000 men are reported to be speeding to reinforce them.

All through last night and today they thundered by in armoured cars and lorries, in goods trains, on horses, and on motor-cycles.

Guns are tonight trained on all roads leading to Austria.

There was alarm in Munich when the news was given for the troop moves that had kept citizens awake all last night.

Women wept as husbands and sons were called to the colours from their jobs.

Municipal buses, beer trucks, commercial lorries were commandeered and loaded with soldiers, guns, pontoons, field kitchens and bridge-building equipment.

'STAND READY'

At the same time the Nazi formations in Munich—storm troops and black guards—were summoned to stand prepared to support the army.

Young men were even recalled from a circus performance last night.

Along Hitler's new motor road from Munich to Austria went a

► PAGE TWO, COL. FIVE

Flashes From Europe

FRANCE'S Chargé d'Affaires in Rome asked the Italian Government whether there was any possibility of France and Italy co-operating on the Austrian question. He was told: "There is no such possibility at present."

ITALY'S Fascist Grand Council, under the presidency of Mussolini, met in Rome last night to discuss the Austrian crisis.
A Government spokesman said: "We shall maintain full diplomatic reserve in view of a delicate and grave situation."

SWITZERLAND reinforced her guards on the Austrian frontier.

LEON BLUM, French Socialist leader, will form a National Government today. He said last night: "I have been pressed by events in Austria." Firm action over Austria is expected.

CZECHO-SLOVAKIA'S Premier Hodza called an extraordinary meeting of the Cabinet. President Benes attended.

Big Fight Weigh-In Ends In A Scuffle

Daily Express Staff Reporter
NEW YORK, Friday.

JOE GOULD, manager for Tommy Farr, almost caused a riot in the dressing-room in Madison-square Garden today when Max Baer and the British heavy-weight champion were weighing in for their fight tonight.

Farr and Baer were posing placidly for photographs when Gould yelled towards Baer and this trainer, Izzy Kline.

Kline stepped in to protect Max and in another second the entire room was filled with struggling, shouting men.

The mob scene lasted half a minute.

Baer's film-star smile faded. Neither he nor Farr—a very grim Farr—took part in the mêlée. But there were no more pictures.

Farr walked away quickly. Baer adjusted his claret and blue woollen tam-o'-shanter at a jaunty angle and said quietly, "Say, who's fighting tonight—me and Farr, or Joe and Izzy?"

BOTH VERY FIT

Gould was still muttering against Baer when the entire ceremony of weighing-in was over. Both men looked exceedingly fit.

Farr weighed fourteen stone twelve and a half pounds; Baer fifteen stone two pounds. Dr. William Walker said that of all the times he had examined Baer he had never been fitter.

Baer's pulse rate was sixty-five to seventy-two, Farr's sixty-eight to seventy-five. Farr was quieter than I have ever seen him. He merely said: "I'll win—you can be sure of that."

Baer, still the smiling playboy in appearance, strutted about saying, "Boys, it's in the bag. It's a cinch."

Two odds shortly before the fight favoured Farr at seven to five, but the general opinion remained that the result was a toss-up, with anything likely to happen.

The loudest voice in New York was Gould's, who yelled up and down the Garden: "Tommy Farr is the next world champion. He can't miss." Farr wagered £100 on himself to win.

Poison Tablets Left On Bus Seat

Hove (Sussex) police were still trying late last night to trace a box of hyoscine tablets which had been left on a bus seat during the day by a nursing home sister.
Chief Constable William C. Hillier had issued a warning that the tablets were poisonous.

Bomb Wrecks Army Recruiting Offices

A bomb exploded in the Army recruiting offices in Alfred-street, Belfast, shortly before midnight. The windows were blown out and the offices wrecked.
No one was injured.

AIR BID TODAY

Jim Broadbent, the airman, planned last night to made a dawn start today from Lympne on his attempt to beat Jean Batten's England-Australia solo flight record of 5 days 18hrs. 3mins.

Fine, Dry

Fine, dry, and fairly warm week-end is forecast. Fine weather area extends from John o' Groats to coast of France.

A GREED damages of £5,000 and 4,000 guineas costs against her former employers were awarded yesterday at the conclusion of the suit brought by Mrs. Frances Lowick, ex-typist, in which she alleged malicious prosecution. Mrs. Lowick returned to her father's home after the case—picture above—and last night told her story to the Daily Express.—See Page Thirteen.

Torse: Button Gives Clue

A PLUM-COLOURED button from a woman's coat, formerly regarded as an insignificant clue, has now become important in the torso mystery. It has led to police restarting dragging operations at Haw Bridge, near Cheltenham.
Report on Page Thirteen.

Daily Herald

No. 6274   •   WEDNESDAY, MARCH 25, 1936   ONE PENNY

QUEEN MARY HEADS FOR OPEN SEA

Ribbentrop Delivers Hitler's Message

HITLER'S envoy returned to London by air from Berlin yesterday and saw Mr. Eden. He brought a message from Hitler discussing in detail Germany's objections to the Locarno Powers' proposals.

He announced that Hitler would submit counter-proposals next Tuesday, after the German elections.—See Page 11.

Sentences on 13 of the 30 Socialists accused of high treason were passed by the Vienna Court yesterday, the others being acquitted—See Page 14.

VERY MILD
(See Page Two)

CERTIFIED DAILY NET
SALE EXCEEDS 2,000,000

Shepherded By Tugs Down The Clyde

THIS aerial picture shows the Queen Mary starting on her first voyage from Clydebank to Southampton yesterday, and enables one to realise the size and beautiful lines of the new pride of the Seven Seas.

Last night the liner anchored off Greenock. She was brilliantly lit up and her searchlights played on the surrounding hills.

Other wonderful pictures are on Page Nine and the Back Page, and the account of our special correspondent on board the Queen Mary will be found on Page Eight.

MARCH

---

19 MONDAY

St Patrick's Day
Holiday, Northern Ireland and Republic of Ireland
New Moon

---

20 TUESDAY

---

21 WEDNESDAY

Vernal Equinox

---

22 THURSDAY

---

23 FRIDAY

---

24 SATURDAY

---

25 SUNDAY

British Summertime begins
First Quarter

Daily Herald, Wednesday, 25 March 1936: the *Queen Mary* sails from the River Clyde to Southampton.

MARCH ~ APRIL

26 MONDAY

27 TUESDAY

28 WEDNESDAY

29 THURSDAY

30 FRIDAY

31 SATURDAY

1 SUNDAY   *Palm Sunday*

The Guardian, Tuesday, 31 March 1981: an assassination attempt on President Reagan.

THE GUARDIAN

Printed in London and Manchester

Tuesday March 31 1981

20p

President jokes on his way to surgery • Oil chief's son arrested • Press aide critically injured

Gunman wounds Reagan in the chest

THE MOMENTS OF AGONY: President Reagan reacts as the shots are fired by the gunman outside the Hilton hotel in Washington yesterday

From Alex Brummer in Washington

President Reagan was last night recovering in hospital after a successful two-hour operation to remove a single bullet from his left lung following an assassination attempt outside the Hilton Hotel, in the centre of Washington.

Dr Dennis O'Leary, a spokesman for the George Washington University Hospital, said the President was awake and in a "stable condition." He said there had been no serious danger to the President's life.

Dr O'Leary said the bullet had ricocheted off his seventh rib. But he assured the American people that the 70-year-old President was in "excellent" condition and in good physical shape.

Three other men were seriously wounded in the shooting. They were the President's 40-year-old press secretary, Mr James Brady, a Washington policeman, and a secret service agent.

Dr O'Leary said last night that a bullet had passed through Mr Brady's brain and he had experienced severe brain injury.

According to the doctors, Mr Reagan had been given a blood transfusion on his arrival at the hospital and before going into surgery. The bullet was found to be lodged in the tissue of the lung and was easily removed because there was no abdominal bleeding. The doctors suggested that Mr Reagan could be up and about again within a fortnight.

More pictures and American assassination attempts, page 5

The doctor said that Mr Reagan had "sailed through the operation" for a man of his age. But he warned that an operation of the kind he had been through causes "stress" to the body, although in Mr Reagan's case, because of his good physical condition, the doctor did not seem unduly concerned.

The White House said the President was in good spirits as he was wheeled into surgery which started at about 4 p.m. local time (10 p.m. BST). He told Senator Paul Laxalt. "Don't worry about me, I'll make it."

A doctor said the President had told Mrs Reagan: "Honey, I forgot to duck," and that he joked with surgeons, "Please tell me you're Republicans." He looked up at assembled aides and said, "Who's minding the store?"

At his bedside was the First Lady, Mrs Nancy Reagan, who shouted to the crowd, "He's all right" as she entered the hospital.

Washington was stunned by the quick sequence of events and affairs on Capitol Hill were immediately halted. The vice-president, Mr George Bush, flew back from Fort Worth, in Texas, and last night took charge of the US government from the White House. However, there seemed to be no suggestion that the authority of the government would pass to Mr Bush.

Apart from Mr. Brady, the other men shot were a secret-service agent, Tim McCarthy, and a Washington policeman, Thomas Delahantey. They were also said to be in a serious condition.

The Secretary of State, Mr Alexander Haig, took control of the government soon after the incident, awaiting the arrival in Washington of the vice-president, Mr George Bush.

Speaking from the White House, Mr Haig said he had been in touch with America's friends and allies abroad to keep them informed on the situation.

Mr Haig soon assembled leading government officials in the White House. They included the Defence Secretary, Mr Caspar Weinberger, the Treasury Secretary, Mr Donald Regan, and the Attorney-General, Mr William French Smith, a close personal friend of Mr Reagan.

Mr Haig looked shaken as he read the statement in a broken voice, saying that no defence alert had been taken.

In the pandemonium outside the Washington Hilton after the shooting, secret service men wrestled the assailant to the ground. He was named as John Warnock Hinckley, aged 25, of Evergreen, Colorado.

He was immediately taken into custody and the secret service said later that Hinckley seemed to have acted alone in his assassination attempt using a 0.22 revolver.

Mr Hinckley, a former disc jockey, apparently attended the Highland Park High School in Dallas.

He will be charged in Washington magistrates' court with the "attempted assassination of the president of the United States."

There was also some confusion about whether the gunman had acted alone or not. The Secretary of State, Mr Alexander Haig declined to answer when asked if there had been a conspiracy. Fuel for this speculation was added when a secret service detail was assigned to Senator Baker.

In a surprise announcement

Turn to back page, col. 4

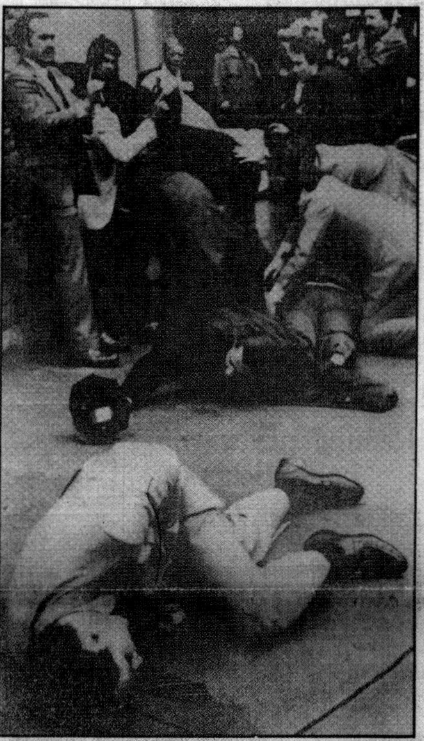

WOUNDED TRIO: Press secretary James Brady (back), policeman (centre) and a secret service agent (front) sprawl on ground

Americans numbed as word spreads

From Jane Rosen in New York

It was raining in New York when the news about the President hit. In many cases, it was the women, at home with their kids, who first heard what happened when radio soap operas were interrupted by the flash. All over town housewives phoned their husbands: "The President's been shot!" "No!"

Astonishingly, the word spread only gradually. By 4.30p.m. people were gathering in anxious little groups on the wet streets to exchange bits of information. Reporters trying to interview passers-by were in turn quizzed for information.

On 58th Street, a man said to no one in particular: "He can't be too badly off, he walked into the hospital." A woman said: "Oh, that's what they tell you — how do you know he really walked?"

Secretary-General Waldheim of the UN was having his monthly luncheon with the Security Council at the East German mission on Park Avenue. When an aide telephoned the mission he could not even get through to Mr Waldheim until he told the shocked operator the news.

Mr Waldheim and the Council members left at once to rush back to the UN.

At St Patrick's Cathedral on 5th Avenue, a crowd of tourists was listening to a lecture when somebody went up to the altar to ask for prayers for the President's recovery. The tourists listened dumbstruck. "What a terrible thing for this country!" an old lady said over and over again.

The Stock Exchange heard the news and within a minute stocks fell three points. Almost 20 years ago, when President John F. Kennedy was assassinated, the market crashed some 30 points.

Yesterday, before that could happen, officials suspended trading and closed the Exchange ten minutes early.

'Nice kid' with oil-rich parents who stunned the world

THE SUSPECT: John W. Hinckley, the arrested man

By Philip Jordan

John Hinckley, the 25-year-old man said to have shot President Reagan, comes from a middle-class family in Evergreen, a suburb of Denver, Colorado. His father is the head of an oil and gas exploration firm.

Hinckley, who has no previous police record, was first brought up in Dallas, Texas. He attended the affluent Highland Park high school in a suburb of Dallas, ironically the city where President John Kennedy was shot dead in 1963. Hinckley went to Colorado when his father's company moved to Denver in 1974. He had briefly attended Yale University.

Neighbours said last night they were shocked to hear of John Hinckley's arrest. They described him as "a nice kid" who they thought was on holiday in California.

His father, Mr John "Jack" Hinckley, learned of the shooting and his son's arrest while at work at the Vanderbilt Energy Corporation of which he is chiarman. "He did not react at all," said Mr Arnold Bjork, the company treasurer. "He just wanted to listen to the radio.

"But there were no other stories about it, so he went home to be with his wife," said Mr Bjork. FBI agents went to the company offices to try to find Mr Hinckley but he had already left for the family home.

Local police said the young Hinckley had no record nor was there any record of mental instability. Mr Hinckley Snr and his wife, Joanne, have another son, Scott, who also works for Vanderbilt.

The principal of Hinckley's former school said there was nothing to make him stick in the memory. But a check of the school yearbook showed that he had belonged to three school clubs, with interests in youth in government, radio and the rodeo.

Hijack plane stormed

From Nicholas Cumming-Bruce in Bangkok

Commandos stormed the Indonesian airliner yesterday where five heavily-armed hijackers were holding 55 hostages.

First reports from Thai police at the scene said two people were killed, and at least three commandos and several passengers on the plane were wounded.

It was not immediately known if the two reported killed were hijackers, hostages, or soldiers.

Witnesses said the troops marched slowly in two-lines, carrying four ladders, across a grassy area toward the Indonesian Airways DC-9, which has been parked on a remote runway at Bangkok's airport for three days.

The attack came a little more than three hours before a 6 a.m. (midnight BST) deadline by which Indonesian officials had agreed to exchange 80 political prisoners for the 55 hostages.

The soldiers put the ladders up against the sides of the aircraft and several mounted on to the wings, the witnesses said. Short bursts of machinegun fire were heard as two doors were forced open. No activity could be seen inside the aircraft as the soldiers entered, leaving one standing on a wing.

A Thai reporter at the scene said several hijackers tried to jump from one of the plane's doors and flee, but were shot by the soldiers. The report could not be confirmed. Officials have made no comment on the attack.

Ambulances drove up to the rear of the plane and some people were taken to local hospitals, the witnesses said. Then a large, bus-like ambulance drove up and the rest of the hostages boarded it and were driven away.

The hijackers, who had pre-

Turn to back page, col. 8

"Pretty boring and predictable questions really: marital status, job, how do we get to work, have we ever tried to stage a coup or been members of the KGB . . . ?"

Solidarity calls off general strike

By Michael Simmons

With less than an hour to go before their final deadline, leaders of the Polish free trade union, Solidarity, last night called off the national strike which the Government had warned would be "catastrophic" in its consequences.

The strike, which would have paralysed the country's bankrupt economy for an indefinite period, was to have started this morning. It would have been without precedent anywhere in Eastern Europe and would have left the Government of General Jaruzelski no choice but to impose a state of emergency.

The decision to cancel, taken after seven hours of talks with the Deputy Prime Minister, Mr Mieczyslaw Rakowski, and after a number of seeming compromises from a Government only too willing to step back from the brink, will throw up as many problems as it resolves.

In the agreement, announced by the official media after seven hours of tense negotiations yesterday, the Government undertook to:

Try to punish individuals responsible for the Bydgoszcz beatings; withdraw immediately special police units from Bydgoszcz, where militant farmers have occupied a public building to press for union right;

Establish a special commission to study the farmers' case and submit proposals by April 5;

Examine demands for the dismissal of the Bydgoszcz deputy governor; guarantee Solidarity's security; pay in full the workers who struck on Friday.

The union in turn accepted a number of Government points. According to a joint communique, Solidarity undertook to:

Accept that there was some justification for the police intervention in Bydgoszcz because there was a climate of extreme tension in the city; halt actions which produced tension, including the occupation of public buildings; enter into negotiations to create mechanisms for settling disputes without rousing the entire nation.

Mr Walesa told the reporters that he was tired of leading Solidarity and said he wanted to quit once the union was firmly established. He has made similar remarks before.

In the short run it represents a personal triumph for the more moderate policies of Solidarity's chairman, Lech Walesa, but in the longer term presents the Soviet Union with an acute dilemma.

Soviet hostility towards Solidarity has been increasing dramatically in the last few days as the union and the Government stepped gingerly from confrontation to confrontation. The Soviet Government news agency, Tass, reported on Sunday — as Poland's political leaders, Mr Rakowski included, were meeting — that the country was "extremely tense" and it gave the impression that the union was running riot throughout the country.

The Russians do not tend to eat their words, and it is fair to assume they will now be watching Polish developments even more closely than before. The Warsaw Pact exercises are

Turn to back page, col. 4

Selwyn likes a bit of magic on the side PAGE 15

The Misery of the Moor Rosalie Shann exclusive PAGE 9

Why the factory Romeo lost his job PAGE 9

ST ON

10

Sun top

Two brutes and a little girl

By BARRY POWELL

THE mother of a four-year-old girl wept tears of rage as she talked of two men who molested her child.

One was jailed for three years for raping and indecently assaulting the girl. The other got two years for indecent assault.

"Ten years should have been the minimum for that monster and his friend," the young mother told me.

"My child still wakes up screaming nine months after it all happened.

"When I or my husband try to comfort her she doesn't know who we are for quite a time.

"Her mind is scarred by these attacks.

"I'd like to kill those two men, I'd like to see them dead for what they did to my baby."

Admitted

The 22-year-old rapist, Raymond Donner, was sentenced by Mr Justice Kilner Brown at Nottingham Crown Court in February.

Conner, of Chance Drive, St Giles, Lincoln, admitted the rape and indecent assault.

John Chapman, 21, of Showbery Gardens, Birchwood, Lincoln, was sentenced at the same court last week

CHAPMAN : He risks violence in jail

by Mr Justice Hutchinson for indecent assault. He denied the charge.

Lincoln police have been shaken by the leniency of the men's sentences.

One senior officer told me : "It's very difficult to explain to junior officers how their diligence and hard work has shown such poor results.

"There is already within police forces up and down the country great frustration about light sentences of this kind.

"This is one of the reasons why more police are leaving the force than are being recruited each year."

Mr James Jardine, chairman of the Police Federation, told me : "For a long time we have been advocating much more severe sentences for assaults of this kind.

Lynch

"Police officers who investigate these crimes see the results.

"In this case, when you bear in mind the age of the girl, it amazes me that the men got only three and two years."

Mr Kenneth Kavanagh, a senior probation

TRIPLE RUM!

And let's raise a glass to Charlotte

HE'S done it again! Red Rum, the Aintree wonder horse, made history yesterday — winning the News of the World Grand National for the third time. And excited fans rushed on to the course in delight as he romped home 25 lengths clear of Churchtown Boy (20-1), Eyecatcher (18-1) and The Pilgarlic (40-1).

It was Rummy's fifth National. In addition to his 1973 and 1974 victories he was runner-up in 1975 and 1976. Jockey Tommy Stack said after yesterday's triumph: "No joking—Red Rum will be heading for the winning post again next year." And last night bookies were already quoting him at 20-1.

HATS OFF to Charlotte Brew, the 21-year-old girl jockey who made it the first National. Odds against her

She was determined to finish the 30-fence course. But Barony Fort refused at the 27th, just four from home, and Charlotte had reluctantly to give up.

WHAT a fantastic race the Grand National is! Talk about thrills. I'm going to keep coming back. You won't be able to keep me away.

The atmosphere on the course is electric. You get caught up in it. I know it sounds crazy, but I had no nerves at all when I came up to the start.

It was far more nerve-racking in the paddock before the race.

It's such a small area and there were so many horses. And everybody is looking at you.

The parade past the stands was an ordeal too, because Barony Fort doesn't like being led and he was raring to go. He could sense the excitement.

Although I've come in for a lot of criticism, nearly all of the jockeys turned to me at the starting gate to wish me luck.

And the crowd kept shouting: "Come on, Char-

lotte." It just made everything more exciting.

I didn't have time to be nervous. Before I knew it, we were away.

They went off at a fantastic pace. And Baron, who is fairly slow, was already in the rear. But

FANTASTIC, I'LL BE BACK TO TRY AGAIN

that's where I wanted him to be.

If I was able to keep him on the outside, out of the way.

Before you know it, the first fence is in front of you. You don't have time to think about it. I saw a lot of horses go down in front of me at the first fence.

Then we were over the second and we settled down into our stride.

The third is the one I was most worried about. It's far more difficult than it looks.

But I was beginning to really love to ride him. As we approached the fourth from home, he was travelling too slowly and approached the fence slightly wrong. Suddenly we were both in the ditch together.

SHOUT

Coming into Valentine's for the first time, Baron jumped it straight as a die. It was passed in a flash.

We came into the Canal turn and I could see horses looking at loose horses running past. I had to shout to him to concentrate on the fence, because I don't think he was looking at it properly.

The Chair was my worst moment. There were three horses milling around. One almost came across in front of me and I was nearly pushed out.

But every time we jumped a fence there was a cheer from the crowd and I really felt I was doing it for them.

All the way round, Baron jumped superbly. I let him pick his stride. He just flew

Becher's and Valentine's the second time round.

But I was beginning to really love him. It was quite hard, but he loved it.

If he'd had horses in front of him, he'd have gone on more.

It's hard pushing a horse on over those kind of fences, especially when he's tiring.

Even so, I thought we would finish.

But then, coming into the fourth from home, he was travelling too slowly and approached the fence slightly wrong. Suddenly we were both in the ditch together.

For a second, we were squashed up against the fence.

I didn't fall off and he was up in a flash. But it was too much to ask him to carry on.

So I pulled him up and trotted back with one of the jockeys who had caught a loose horse.

By this time, I knew that Red Rum had won the race and I was tremendously thrilled about it.

I'm really disappointed that I didn't finish, but after this experience, there's no doubt about it — I'll be back again.

My only real worry was Baron getting hurt.

To me he's my one and only.

If anything had happened to him, I don't know what I'd have done or how I'd have felt.

But he loves the course and he loves the race. So I'll definitely be back next year.

My parents bought Baron for me as a Christmas present four years ago. He has been the only horse for me ever since.

What I'd really like is a faster Baron.

I proved all my critics wrong. I've proved that I'm fit enough and experienced to ride the course. I've proved that I'm no trouble to other riders.

Now my one ambition is to win the National.

DIET

AFTER the race Charlotte celebrated with chocolate cake and champagne — a change from her diet for the last week.

But she loves the course and be has been in strict training.

People who doubted her toughness—like some of her fellow - jockeys — didn't know that at that time she was riding with a broken nose and cracked ribs.

Charlotte and her mother drove from their home in Coggeshall, Essex, with Barony Fort on Wednesday to prepare for yesterday's race.

While many other jockeys

Continued on Page 2

Your pa rise lim —a five

CHANCELLOR Denis Healey is firm on a £5 pay plan. He will tough stance in negotiations with in the next few weeks.

Any flexibility or restoration of tials will have to be within that And the hard line must lead to a clash with union chiefs like Jack Joe Gormley and Clive Jenkins.

They are looking for a deal to at least keep pace with the 16 per cent cost of living increase in the past year.

But the Chancellor is determined that the total pay boost under the Stage 3 policy will be under 10 per cent.

He reckons he has already raised takehome pay four per cent by raising tax allowances and promising to slash five per cent off the 35 per cent standard rate of income tax if the unions play ball.

So actual pay rises must be kept below six per cent when the new deal comes into force in August.

Mr Healey plans to inject flexibility into the new deal. It will include pay bargaining at factory level, with management and unions deciding how the kitty should be shared.

Differentials

In that way, some differentials could be restored.

But he has not ruled out such deals, he believes they are open to such deals, he believes they are open to abuse and phoney claims.

Another blow to union hopes will be Mr Healey's refusal of a general prices freeze.

Social Services Secretary David Ennals underlined the Government's tough mood on pay in a speech at Durham yesterday.

He said : "We want a bit of room to manoeuvre on the wages cake within the baking tin while it is cooking.

APRIL

2 MONDAY

Full Moon

3 TUESDAY

Passover (Pesach), First Day

4 WEDNESDAY

5 THURSDAY

Maundy Thursday

6 FRIDAY

Good Friday
Holiday, UK, Republic of Ireland, Canada,
USA, Australia and New Zealand

7 SATURDAY

8 SUNDAY

Easter Sunday

News of the World, Sunday, 3 April 1977: Red Rum wins the Grand National for the third time.

APRIL

---

9 MONDAY

Easter Monday
Holiday, UK (exc. Scotland), Republic of Ireland,
Canada, Australia and New Zealand
Passover (Pesach), Seventh Day

---

10 TUESDAY

Passover (Pesach), Eighth Day
Last Quarter

---

11 WEDNESDAY

---

12 THURSDAY

---

13 FRIDAY

---

14 SATURDAY

---

15 SUNDAY

The Independent, Saturday, 11 April 1998: the Northern Ireland peace agreement is signed at Stormont Castle.

HOW I HOAXED NEW YORK
William Boyd talks to John Walsh
MAGAZINE

NUREYEV, THE GREATEST MALE DANCER
Why his legend should be left alone
ARTS, PAGE 18

THEY CAN'T SAY NO
Why some gay men come unstuck
FEATURES, PAGE 16

THEY DIDN'T STAND A CHANCE
David Aaronovitch on being third class on the Titanic
COMMENT, PAGE 21

THE INDEPENDENT

Newspaper of the Year for photographs

Saturday 11 April 1998 70p No 3,582 ★★★

Blair, Ahern and Mitchell seal historic agreement 17 hours after passing of talks deadline

Peace at last for Ulster

By David McKittrick
Ireland Correspondent

THE PEOPLE of Northern Ireland were offered peace yesterday, with a historic agreement which paved a way out of 30 years of violence.

After a night and day of drama, the exhausted politicians hammered out last-minute differences and produced a potentially ground-breaking document. Tony Blair, the Prime Minister, Bertie Ahern, the Taoiseach, and talks chairman George Mitchell sealed the deal at 5pm yesterday, 17 hours after the midnight deadline.

A great many loose ends remain and many political obstacles lie ahead, but the sense that a new beginning had been made was palpable both at the talks themselves and on the streets of Belfast. A woman who walked through the city centre said: "I saw people with tears in their eyes. I shed a few myself."

They were tears of relief rather than of victory, for the agreement produced yesterday was composed of scores of compromises stitched together in a 69-page document combining points made by the two governments and the eight parties at the table.

The political achievement lies in the production of a document which has been accepted, however tentatively, across a political spectrum ranging from David Trimble's Ulster Unionist Party to Sinn Fein.

Minutes after the deal was agreed, Mr Blair appeared on the steps of Stormont Castle to declare victory: "I believe today courage has triumphed. I said when I arrived here on Wednesday night that I felt the hand of history upon us. Today I hope that the burden of history can at long last start to be lifted from our shoulders."

Mr Blair said that the agreement enshrined fairness and equality for the population of Northern Ireland. But he said: "This will not work unless we extend a hand of friendship to those who were our foes." Echoing these sentiments, Mr Ahern said the agreement was about the promise of a brighter future: "Today we hope a line can be drawn under a bloody past."

Mr Ahern added that his ultimate political aspiration remained the coming together of all the people of Ireland "achieved peacefully and with consent".

The US President, Bill Clinton, intervened during the day with telephone calls which, according to both the Unionists and Sinn Fein, helped overcome a final hurdle. Mr Blair appealed to Mr Clinton to get involved after Mr Trimble demanded "clarification" on the decommissioning of paramilitary weapons.

The republican position was spelt out by Sinn Fein's chief negotiator, Martin McGuinness, who said the party's aim was "to move in a transitional way towards our primary objective of the eventual reunification of Ireland. We will examine this document to establish whether it can move us decisively in that direction".

He added: "Sinn Fein hasn't signed up to anything. Sinn Fein in the course of the coming days will consider and reflect on the contents of the document. We will have our own debates and discussions, be in touch with our grassroots, and at the end of that comprehensive process of dialogue and discussion we will make our position known to the public."

His suggestion that the document might represent a move towards Irish unity was starkly at odds with the view of Mr Trimble, who declared: "I know that I have risen from this table with the union stronger than when I sat down."

Both unionism and republicanism must now sell the agreements to grassroots which will include many with doubts about the new course of give and take which it sketches out.

But in itself it represents a triumph for almost all involved, in particular the local representatives who made a successful transition from the politics of demand to the politics of negotiation.

The official talks deadline had been set as midnight on Thursday, but with no agreement in sight at that point bargaining went on through the night. It was not until late afternoon that an agreed text was completed. At a final session, Mr Mitchell spoke of the "remarkable experience" of his involvement in the peace process. He said: "I have that bitter-sweet feeling that comes in life. I am dying to leave but I hate to go."

The document also envisages potentially dramatic new moves towards releases of paramilitary prisoners, including the increasing of remission from the present one-half to two-thirds. One source said: "If this all falls into place then all the prisoners could be out in two years – three at the most."

Key points of the deal

- A Northern Ireland assembly will have 108 members, elected by proportional representation. It will be run by an executive committee of 12 members.
- The assembly will have powers to legislate, but its first responsibility is to set up a North-South Ministerial Council on issues including cross-border co-operation.
- The Irish government will amend its constitution, which lays claim to the territory of Northern Ireland. In return, London will replace the Government of Ireland Act.
- A further proposal for a Council of the Isles, with members drawn from north and south as well as from the Scottish and Welsh assemblies.
- Agreement to be put to the peoples of Northern Ireland and the Republic in referenda on 22 May.

It's a deal: Bertie Ahern and Tony Blair outside Stormont after striking an agreement on Ulster Photograph: Peter Macdiarmid

Cauldrons of the Troubles yearn for normality

By Andy Buncombe

ON THE litter-strewn Shankill Road there was a sense of calm yesterday evening, broken only by the persistent but ignored ringing of a security alarm. Most shops were shuttered for the night and there were only a few people out.

The settlement, aimed at bringing peace to communities such as the Protestant Shankill, had been delivered a few hours earlier, but details were hazy and most people remained cautious.

"I think it's better than nothing but we are going to have to wait and see how it goes," said Alan Irvine, 26, heading home from the video shop. "We've been at war for the past 30 years and it has got us nowhere." Mr Irvine, a father of two, said he was unlike many of the community's young people, who appeared less interested in the settlement than the older generation. "We will have to wait and reserve our judgement. There have been too many false dawns but everybody wants it to work."

Eileen Turkington, 54, and her friend Ann Donnelly, 49, were heading into the Shankill Methodist Church. Both had lived through the Troubles and both were hopeful the settlement could bring peace. "People are browned off. Most of us just want to have a peaceful life without living in fear," said Mrs Turkington.

"As it is at the moment people are afraid to go out." Two doors down from the church stood the remains of a chip shop, destroyed in the early 1990s by a bomb. Four, five or maybe more people were killed by the republican atrocity; the ladies could not remember.

The Shankill Road of West Belfast runs largely parallel to the Catholic Falls Road, and not just geographically.

While in the Falls Road you find the republican tricolour, here flies the Union flag; in the Falls Road the street murals show the IRA, while here the paintings of the masked men represent the UVF.

Parallel but close. On the Falls Road most people you meet are fed up with violence, on the Shankill Road most people also yearn for peace.

Jean Whiteside, 68, sat staring out of the window of her grocery store.

"There are an awful lot of decent people here who are not interested in the paramilitaries," said Mrs Whiteside, who has 12 grandchildren. "I don't want violence for my grandchildren and I am sure the men with clubs and guns do not want violence for theirs."

INSIDE
The historic agreement, page 2
Deal not possible without Clinton, page 3
The long road to peace, page 17
Andrew Marr, page 21
Leading article, page 20

Four feared dead in worst flooding for a century

By Kate Watson-Smyth

TWO PEOPLE died and another two, including a 14-year-old boy, were missing yesterday as torrential rain brought the worst flooding for a century to parts of Britain.

The body of a middle-aged man was recovered from a flooded caravan park on the banks of the Avon near Evesham after the floods left hundreds of people homeless. And a woman was found dead, believed drowned, in a badly flooded part of Northampton.

Police and firefighters carried out a series of rescue operations across the Midlands, Buckinghamshire and Oxfordshire as forecasters predicted more rain at the start of the Easter weekend.

Norman Edgington, regional manager of the National Rivers Authority, said: The flooding in the river Avon area is the worst since records began in 1900 – the river is 15 metres above its normal level."

Firefighters worked round the clock to save people from the River Mead Caravan Park, in Worcestershire, after the river Arrow rose by four metres during the middle of the night and the site was engulfed.

Families huddled together on top of their caravans as water swept through the park, reaching roof level in some parts. Some were winched to safety by helicopter and others were rescued by boat.

One rescue boat struck a submerged tractor and the two firemen and four caravaners were tipped into the swirling water in the pitch darkness, but they were eventually found.

David O'Dwyer, chief of Hereford and Worcester fire service, said all the brigade's 800 firefighters worked round the clock to rescue people. "The water on the caravan sites was at least 6ft deep in places and the river speed is running at 11 knots, which is extremely fast".

In Warwickshire, rescue teams were yesterday searching for a 14-year-old boy who disappeared when a van was swept from a flooded road into a ditch at Eathorpe, near Leamington Spa.

The van was washed into the ditch as it tried to overtake broken-down vehicles stranded in floodwater. It was quickly submerged but the driver managed to climb on to the roof and was eventually rescued by a police officer. The boy could not be found however. Steve West, Warwickshire Ambulance Service's director of operations, described the conditions as "desperate" and said they feared the worst.

Hopes were also fading for a 33-year-old woman believed to have fallen from a narrowboat on a flooded river in Northampton.

More than 300 people were rescued from their homes and moved to emergency centres in Buckingham and Banbury, Oxfordshire, where the torrential rain caused the river Cherwell and the Oxford Canal to merge.

An RAF helicopter was called out to rescue 19 anglers who became stranded in the middle of a lake near Milton Keynes, Buckinghamshire, after the water level rose by 9ft in an hour.

Photograph, page 4

Washout: One man and his dog keeping dry above the floodwaters at Cropredy, near Banbury, Oxfordshire Photograph: David Hartley Pictures

15
9 770951 946566

INSIDE GUIDE: WEATHER, P2 ● CROSSWORDS TIME OFF P14, 28 ● TELEVISION, THE EYE ● FULL CONTENTS, P2

The Daily News

LATE LONDON EDn.

D.N. 20,624. LONDON & MANCHESTER, TUESDAY, APRIL 16, 1912. ONE HALF-PENNY.

TITANIC GOES DOWN OFF CAPE RACE.

Wrecked by Collision with an Iceberg.

MANY LIVES LOST.

Others Saved by Liners Summoned by Wireless.

Telegrams received in London at two o'clock this morning reveal the fact that the loss of the great White Star liner Titanic off Cape Race after collision with an iceberg has been accompanied by loss of life.

Earlier telegrams stated that all the passengers and crew had been saved, and an official message indicated that all on board were removed to the boats before the Titanic disappeared beneath the waves.

Later, however, the officials of the White Star Line in New York admitted that many lives had been lost.

There is much conflict between official and unofficial statements, but it now appears clear that the Titanic struck an iceberg six hundred miles from land at 10.25 on Sunday night (3.25 yesterday morning English time), and foundered at 2.20 a.m. (7.20 a.m. English time).

The Titanic, which cost £1,250,000, was on her maiden voyage.

Among those on board, who with the crew numbered 2,358, were Mr. J. Bruce Ismay, of the White Star Line, Mr. W. T. Stead, Col. J. J. and Mrs. Astor, Countess Rothes, Mr. C. M. Hays, President of the Grand Trunk Railway of Canada, Mr. and Mrs. M. Rothschild, Mr. Christopher Head, formerly Mayor of Chelsea, and a large number of other well-known people. A list of saloon passengers is printed elsewhere.

It was at 3.25 yesterday morning that the signal "S.O.S." was circulated from the Marconi room of the Titanic. The Allan liner Virginian, steaming 170 miles away, first answered the call, and flashed news of the disaster to Montreal, whence it was transmitted to New York and London, as she raced to the rescue.

Other ocean liners picked up the call for aid, and within a few minutes vessels representing many nationalities were on the way to the scene of the disaster. Among them were the Olympic—the Titanic's sister ship—the Baltic, and three or four German and French liners.

At 3.55 a.m. the Virginian reported the receipt of a message from the Titanic stating that the vessel was going down by the head, and that the women and children were being transferred to the lifeboats.

Only brief wireless accounts of the disaster have been received, and full details cannot be known until the survivors have landed.

APPALLING NEWS.

Messages Indicate very Heavy Loss of Life.

NEW YORK, Monday.

Six hundred and fifty-five of the Titanic's passengers and crew are known to have been saved. It is feared that the others have been lost.—Central [illegible]

NEW YORK, April 15, 8.20 p.m.

The following statement has been given out by the White Star officials:

Captain Haddock, of the Olympic, sends a wireless message that the Titanic sank at 2.20 a.m. Monday, after all the passengers and crew had been lowered into lifeboats and transferred to the Virginian.

The steamer Carpathia, with several hundred passengers from the Titanic, is now on her way to New York.—Reuter.

8.40 p.m.

The White Star officials now admit that many lives have been lost.—Reuter.

8.45 p.m.

The following dispatch has been received here from Cape Race: "The steamer Olympic reports that the steamer Carpathia reached the Titanic's position at daybreak, but found boats and wreckage only. She reported that the Titanic foundered about 2.20 a.m. in latitude 41 degrees 16 minutes, longitude 50 degrees 14 minutes."

The message adds: "All the Titanic's boats are accounted for. About 675 souls have been saved of the crew and passengers. The latter are nearly all women and children.

"The Leyland liner California is remaining and searching the vicinity of the disaster. The Carpathia is returning to New York with the survivors."—Reuter.

(From Our Own Correspondent.)

NEW YORK, Monday Night.

Civilized communities in this hemisphere, no less than in the Old World, were stunned by to-day's news that the White Star liner Titanic, the greatest ocean vessel afloat, while on her maiden voyage had collided with an iceberg, and was sinking at sea 600 miles off Nova Scotia.

The story seemed incredible, and the White Star offices, as well as the Marconi headquarters, in this city were overwhelmed by an avalanche of inquiries. For nearly twelve hours they had no news.

The first wireless intimation was sent by the Marconi operator on board the Titanic, and sent on from Cape Race. First came the famous call for aid made historic by Binns of Republic memory three years ago. Then came the news, couched in vivid phrase and without circumlocution:

> **"Have struck an iceberg 41.46 north, 50.14 west. Are badly damaged. Rush aid."**

The morning papers all printed this message, and upon it they based four or five columns containing highly imaginative conjectures and elaborate details of the icefields which the Carmania, only forty-eight hours before, had encountered. Pictures of the Titanic on end, compared with the Eiffel Tower and the Singer skyscraper, a full list of the first saloon passengers, and portraits of Mr. and Mrs. J. J. Astor, Major Butt, President Taft's aide-de-camp, and Mr. W. T. Stead completed the effort.

There had been great interest in the Titanic's first trip, just as there was when her sister ship, the Olympic, crossed a year ago, and just as there always is in New York when new Transatlantic leviathans are nearing these shores.

It was stated only yesterday that wireless reported her 1,284 miles from Sandy Hook, and that she might reach port at four o'clock on Tuesday afternoon. This would have beaten the Olympic's initial record last year.

It was not until past eleven o'clock that official intelligence was received here in the form of the following wireless message [illegible], eastward bound on the Olympic:

> "Am 260 miles away. Parisian and Carpathia in attendance on Titanic. Carpathia has taken off 20 boatloads of women and children. Calm sea. Baltic approaching."

This news relieved anxiety, which had been almost beyond description.

The Carpathia's destination was the Mediterranean, but it was assumed that she would return to land the rescued passengers at Halifax.

The next wireless message said:

> Virginian arrived. Has thrown line, and is about to tow disabled liner 600 miles to Halifax.

It is unofficially added that the Virginian was not the only Allan liner which aided in the rescue, for the Parisian was alongside before her sister ship had started preparations for acting as tug, and was helping herself to all the human cargo the Cunarder could not accommodate.

CROWDED RESCUE SHIPS.

Further unofficial messages state that the Parisian and the Carpathia, crowded to the rails with survivors, left the stricken liner soon after noon, and headed for Halifax, whence the passengers will be brought to New York by rail.

When the Baltic hove in sight the Cunarder and the Allan vessel had started, but the Baltic, which, singularly enough, performed a similar service for the Republic's passengers in January, 1909, taking them off the Florida, was sent in hot pursuit with the purpose of transferring the survivors, so as to enable them to reach Halifax perhaps half a day earlier.

Telegraphic orders for sleeping cars for 600 and ordinary carriages for 800 had already been dispatched to the Maine Central Railway.

Later messages stated that the Titanic's bulkheads forward were holding up well. Most of the crew of 900 remained on board, as the chances of reaching port were regarded as good.

As the vessels laden with survivors got into touch with the wireless stations ashore hundreds of messages, including Transatlantic cablegrams from the London "Daily News" and the London "Daily Telegraph," were sent to the Carpathia. The Titanic's wireless apparatus was evidently out of commission, for the brief messages sent ashore came either from the Carpathia or the Parisian.

BADLY DAMAGED.

Several coast stations reported having received unidentified messages, saying that the Titanic was very badly damaged, but all efforts to induce the captains of both the Titanic and the Olympic to say precisely to what extent were unavailing.

There will be thrilling tales to tell when Halifax is reached to-morrow night, and most of the messages for Titanic passengers are unlikely to gain their destination until the Baltic anchors in Halifax Harbour. Nor is it probable, in view of the limited Marconi range, that anyone on board the smaller White Star boat will succeed in getting more than tabloid tidings to English or American friends before to-morrow.

One can picture the Olympic's frantic efforts to get into touch with her sister in distress. In the small hours of the morning, when 220 miles away, she Marconied to Cape Race:

> Am using every ounce of steam on both turbine and reciprocating engines.

It was about this time, while the Titanic and the Virginian were interchanging signals, that the wireless operator on the latter reported that the Titanic's signals became blurred and then ceased.

Early in the afternoon Montreal had sent the "news" that the Titanic had sunk, but the White Star officials refused to believe it. "We much prefer," they said, "the real intelligence coming from the Virginian's wireless operator."

25 ICEBERGS.

Narrow Escapes of Other Liners.

(From Our Own Correspondent.)

NEW YORK, Monday Night.

Steamship company officials, usually the keenest business rivals, have been sympathetic in the highest degree. Scores of them have called at the White Star headquarters to inquire about the great ship. Had she been their own they could not have been more solicitous.

Captain Jameson, of the American liner St. Paul, sister ship of the New York, which the Titanic had sucked [illegible] she started her maiden voyage, dropped in to give what cheer he could.

"It would be easier to sink a cork than the Titanic with her fifteen watertight bulkheads," he said. "You could break her into three pieces, and every one of 'em would stay afloat."

Interesting news of the ice field into which the Titanic ran was brought by the Carmania yesterday. She herself had a perilous time. So had the French liner Niagara, and several smaller liners have been caught and badly damaged.

Passengers on the Cunarder say they saw a fleet of twenty-five enormous bergs as the ship steamed by dead slow. Captain Dow constantly blew his siren, for the bergs were so big they could easily have hidden another liner a few hundred yards away.

The captain told the reporters he had "never seen so much ice before. Ice was on all sides of us, trembling, undulating, and rasping, and every once in a while we ran into a growler."

"What's a growler?" he was asked.

"It's a piece of ice," he said, "which rams another, and is called the ice growler. We saw one huge plateau berg with a deep green reflection.

"Though I was 70 feet above water there were times when I could see nothing but great masses of ice. As we left this field we ran into a dense fog."

This was last Thursday when the Carmania was off Newfoundland banks.

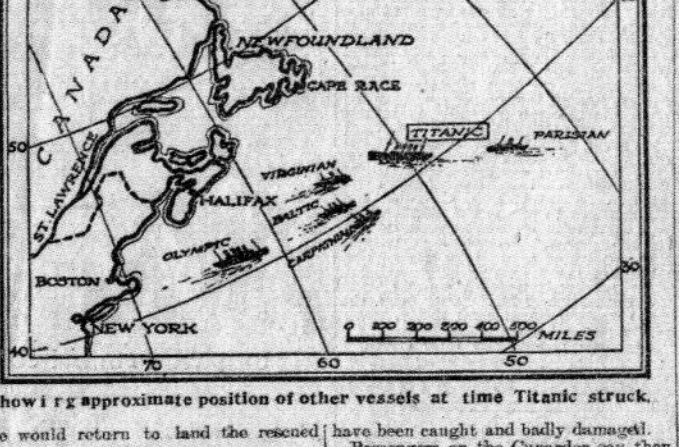

Showing approximate position of other vessels at time Titanic struck.

A REPORT OF PANIC.

HALIFAX (N.S.), Monday.

A message was received at two this afternoon stating that the Titanic is being towed to Halifax by the Allan liner Virginian. Her passengers are expected to arrive her on Wednesday, and arrangements for their conveyance to New York are proceeding rapidly. No direct news has yet been received from the Titanic's captain.

It is stated that there was some tendency towards panic among the passengers during the first few moments after the collision, but that the majority of them behaved admirably.

Salvage tugs are preparing to go out and assist the Virginian in bringing the Titanic into port. It is believed that not a single life has been lost.—Central News.

BORDEAUX, April 15.

A Norwegian steamer has arrived here, and reports having picked up yesterday morning off the Olonne sands the balloon Centaure, which was flying the ensign of the Aero Club of France. There were no passengers in the car. The balloon was slightly damaged, but still inflated.—Reuter.

Titanic starting on her maiden voyage from Southampton. [Topical.

"DON'T WORRY."

Wireless Operator's Message Home.

Mr. and Mrs. G. A. Phillips, of Farncombe, Godalming, parents of the wireless operator on board the Titanic, last night received the following message from their son:

> **Making slowly for Halifax. Practically unsinkable; don't worry.**

Mr. J. G. Phillips, the operator, was appointed to the Titanic for this voyage after having served on the Teutonic, Lusitania, Mauretania, and Oceanic.

Mr. Phillips is 25 years of age, and served as a telegraphist in the Godalming Post Office, afterwards joining the Marconi School at Liverpool.

"UNSINKABLE."

News of the Loss a Blow to the Experts.

The total loss of the Titanic will prove a great disappointment to her owners and builders, who believe[illegible]r unsinkable.

"The Titanic is un[illegible]able. Her bulkhead system is so co[illegible]ete that she cannot possibly go to the [illegible]ttom." That was [illegible] in answer to a [illegible] the possibility of getting the [illegible] to port.

A representative of [illegible] builders informed an interviewe[illegible]sterday that the Titanic's hull was of tre[illegible]endous strength. By means of fifteen tra[illegible]verse bulkheads the hull was divided in[illegible] separate compartments, any two of which might be flooded without danger to the ship.

Each bulkhead was [illegible]ed with watertight doors, those giving communication between the various boiler rooms and engine rooms being arranged on the drop system.

"Each door," said th[illegible] official description, "is held in the open position by a suitable friction clutch, which can be instantly released by means of a powerful electric magnet controlled from the captain's bridge, so that, in the event of accident, or at any time when it may be considered advisable, the captain can, by simply moving an electric switch, instantly close the doors throughout, practically making the vessel unsinkable.

"Moreover, as a further precaution, floats are provided beneath the floor level, which, in the event of water accidentally entering any of the compartments, automatically lift and thereby close the doors opening into that compartment if they have not already been dropped by those in charge of the vessel.

"A ladder or escape is provided in each boiler-room, engine-room, and similar watertight compartment, in order that the closing of the doors at any time shall not imprison the men working therein; though the risk of this eventuality is lessened by electric bells placed in the vicinity of each door, which ring prior to their closing, and thus give warning to those below."

It is thus plain that the Titanic's chances of reaching port depended upon the strength of the bulkheads in the flooded fore compartments. Probably the Virginian towed the crippled ship stern first in order to minimise the strain—the plan which was adopted, it will be remembered, when one-half of the Suevic, another White Star boat, was towed round to Southampton after the ship had been wrecked at the Lizard.

CAPTAIN SMITH.

Master Who Commanded the Olympic.

Captain E. J. Smith, R.N.R., who was in command of the Titanic, is one of the best known and most popular figures on the Atlantic service. He has been particularly unlucky, as he was the captain of the Olympic when that vessel collided with the cruiser Hawke off Cowes last September. He has been a servant of the White Star Line for many years, and has been placed in command of the company's biggest vessels.

Captain Smith, who is sixty years of age, was born in Staffordshire. He served his apprenticeship to the sea with Messrs. Gibson and Co., Liverpool. He joined the White Star Line as fourth officer, and has been one of the company's commanders since 1887.

He was a member of the Executive Council of the Mercantile Marine Service Association prior to his removal to Southampton to take over the command of the Oceanic when the White Star moved their service to the Channel. He holds an extra master's certificate.

Other leading officers of the Titanic are Surgeon W. F. N. O'Loughlin, Assistant-Surgeon J. E. Simpson, Pursers H. W. McElroy and R. L. Barker and Chief Steward A. Latimer.

The majority of the nine hundred men forming the Titanic's crew are either natives of Southampton or are domiciled at that port.

Details of the lost Titanic and the saloon passenger list appear on Page 5.

A CRASH AT NIGHT.

Passengers Sleeping at Time of Disaster.

NEW YORK, Monday Night.

The Titanic struck the iceberg at 10.25 last night (American time). She was then running at reduced speed. Most of the passengers had retired to bed, and were awakened and terrified by a thunderous impact which crushed and twisted the towering bows of the liner and broke them in like an eggshell.

The behaviour of the crew is stated to have been exemplary, and they were assisted by many of the male passengers, who succeeded in calming the women and children.—Central News.

GIANT ICEBERGS.

Perils of the North Atlantic Passage.

With the movement of the ice southwards each year the perils of the Atlantic passages are increased. Ships' captains warn each other of the presence of these *great floating islands, but they are often* hidden by fog—even in broad daylight there may be only a few feet of a monster floe visible above the surface—and there is [illegible]

Monster bergs have been reported in the month of May. The French liner Lorraine saw one in a recent May which was 675ft. high and 1,500ft. long. The steamer Armenian sighted another in June, 1905, in the very neighbourhood from which the urgent calls came from the Titanic, and that berg was 300ft. high and 900ft. long.

Generally the portion of the berg visible above water is only one-eighth or one-ninth of its total depth.

Many ships have been wrecked by these floating monsters. In 1903 20 steamers met with serious accidents through contact with ice near the Banks, and two were totally lost.

In 1879 the liner Arizona drove her stem against a berg almost to the foremast, but floated owing largely to the fact that 300 tons of ice were jammed in her forepeak. She had 650 people on board, but got them all to port.

The City of Berlin, with a company of 700, had a similar experience. In the spring of 1899 ten large tramp steamers were all put on the list of missing, and each of them was in the neighbourhood of the Newfoundland Banks when last heard of. Another bad ice year was 1909, when the ice peril was exceptionally severe.

It is generally believed that two missing liners of the sixties, the City of Washington and the City of Boston, which disappeared with all hands, were lost by collision with icebergs.

INSURANCE RATES.

Owners to Pay First £150,000 Worth of Repairs.

The Titanic was insured at the low rate of 15s. per cent. for £1,000,000 against total loss, while for partial damage there is what is known as an access of £150,000. This means that if the vessel is not a total loss the company bears the cost of the first £150,000 worth of repairs themselves.

When the news of the disaster arrived the reinsurance rates started at 50 guineas, soon rising to 60 guineas, and then fell to 40. On the receipt of the unsigned message stating that the Titanic was proceeding under her own steam to Halifax, there was a further fall to 35 guineas, and then to 30 guineas.

The ship cost £1,250,000 to build, and for insurance purposes her hull is valued at a million.

So far as can be ascertained there is no specie included in the Titanic's cargo, but she was carrying a large number of valuable postal packets.

EFFECT IN WALL STREET.

NEW YORK, April 15.

On the Stock Exchange to-day International Mercantile Marine bonds declined 2 points, with a fall of 4 points in International Mercantile Marine Preferred coincidentally with the report of the disaster to the Titanic.—Reuter.

A RICH CARGO.

NEW YORK, Monday.

According to newspaper reports, the Titanic carried something like £1,000,000 worth of bonds and jewels, etc. All these valuables, it is believed, have been saved.—Central News.

WORLD'S RECORD LINERS.

	Length feet.	Breadth feet.	Gross tons.
Great Eastern (1858) ...	680	82.8	18,915
City of Paris (1889) ...	527.6	63.2	10,670
Kaiser Friedrich (1898)	584	64	12,000
Oceanic (1899) ...	685	68	16,900
Lusitania (1907) ...	790	88	32,000
Olympic (1910) ...	882	92½	45,000
Titanic (1912) ...	882½	92½	45,000
Imperator (prob. 1913)	910	95	50,000

WIRELESS & LIFE-SAVING AT SEA.

WONDERFUL RECORD OF NINE YEARS.

WORLD'S GROWING DEBT OF GRATITUDE.

There can be few men living to-day more entitled to feel they have benefited their day and generation as well as the unborn heirs of the planet than the remarkable band of men in the British Postal Telegraph Service, who, under Sir William Preece, first investigated the mysteries of wireless telegraphy, and Signor Marconi, who made its use commercially possible.

If, as was hoped yesterday, between two and three thousand souls are in safety who, ten short years ago, would have had only the barest chance of surviving the horrors of shipwreck in mid-Atlantic. And all this because one summer's morning in Gray's Inn-road in the early eighties a telephone linesman heard on an overhead line the Morse code messages being transmitted on an insulated cable running under the street a hundred feet below. His pole and wires were properly insulated, and yet [illegible]

Wm. Preece has told how the man came to him to solve the mystery; how they nearly threw away the key at the beginning of the search by trying to stop the wireless transmission; and how at last, finding they could not stop it, they turned it to account in the public service first in Scotland between an island and the mainland when a cable was broken, and then in Wales.

To-day's story of the disaster to the Titanic provides a record in life-saving by wireless. The nine short years since its general adoption after the wreck of the St. Louis in the January of 1903 have, however, been full of instances in which its saving power, if one may put it so, has been demonstrated. It was in December, 1903, that the first use was made of wireless telegraphy in life-saving. On that date the Kroonland, of the Red Star Line, from Antwerp, with 900 passengers on board, encountered a fearful gale 150 miles west of the Fastnet. Her steering-gear was smashed, and the huge ship became a menace to herself and others. On board was a wireless installation, and the C.D.Q. signal for help was sent flashing out over the waters. Crookhaven was first to "pick up" the signals, and in the teeth of the gale tugs were soon on the way to find the liner. In an hour and a half those on board had got their instructions from Antwerp, via Crookhaven, and a few hours after were being towed into Queenstown and safety.

Three months later, in March, 1904, the New York, which had stranded at Cape La Hogue, and in May of that year the Friesland, which was in difficulties through a broken propeller shaft, both found help by the same means. But it is perhaps the case of the liner Republic, in January, 1909, which will be best remembered. One of its effects was to make famous Jack Binns, the wireless operator on board. Outward bound with 761 souls, the Republic, of the White Star Company, was rammed while 70 miles south of Nantucket by the steamship Florida, of the Lloyd Italian Line. With his instrument-room wrecked, Binns stuck to his post, sending out continuously his appeal for succour. Soon it was heard and answered by the sister ship, the Baltic, which arrived hardly more than in time to avert heavy loss of life.

In the October of 1907 the Poulsen apparatus on the ss. Lituania had been instrumental in saving 864 lives when the vessel, crowded with emigrants, ran aground at Skillinge, in the Baltic. The message was picked up at Herr Poulsen's laboratory at Lyngby, near Copenhagen, and in a few hours relief vessels and a salvage boat from the Danish port were alongside. The use of wireless in the recent wreck of the ss. Delhi, and when the Cunard liner, the Slavonia, stranded at Flores, in the Azores, is in every one's mind, as well as the rescue, but a week since, of the passengers and crew of the burning Ontario, bound from Baltimore to Boston. Less sensational, but none the less useful, was the rescue of the disabled C.P.R. liner Montrose in July, 1909. The vessel had collided with an iceberg in a dense fog, and it was wireless brought H.M.S. Brilliant to her aid.

Only a few weeks back the Osterley, thirty hours out of Colombo, homeward bound, met a four-masted steamer on fire and abandoned, drifting in the current between the Red Sea and Colombo, and right in the "steam lane." In a few hours it had become a partially-submerged derelict, a danger and menace to all who do business in the great waters. Before nightfall the Osterley, in reply to wireless messages, learnt that the crew had been saved by a French ship, and had also informed Lloyd's agent at Bombay, and thus warned the shipping of the world of the danger. At the Lizard, at Malin Head, and at other such points many a gallant ship has found in her wireless installation the means of saving her from disaster in the fogs. The time must shortly come when no ship will no more think of sailing without such an installation than of putting to sea without lifeboats. When that day arrives the perils of the great waters will be immeasurably lessened, and the sum of the world's gratitude to the men who discovered and developed the system will, or should be, correspondingly greater.

HOME RULE IN THE HOUSE.

MR. BALFOUR IN GLOOMY MOOD.

ULSTER BOGEY.

SIGNIFICANT SILENCE OF EX-TORY LEADER.

FINANCE REPORT.

STRIKING SUGGESTIONS OF THE COMMITTEE.

From Our Parliamentary Correspondent.

WESTMINSTER, Monday Night.

Mr. Balfour has addressed the House for more than an hour, without one mention of Ulster's terrors. He did, indeed, in a casual phrase speak of "batoning" and bayoneting" Belfast. He dismissed with airy gesture the guarantees, which, he said, were as absurd as the old claims of British monarchs to be "kings of France." But of Rome Rule we had not a syllable. That bogey is laid.

But a larger, more menacing spectre loomed forth—all the more formidable because its outlines were dim and indistinct. "This," said he, his arms outstretched, "is a fair-weather constitution, when the horizon is overcast, when by a dumb instinct the nations are anxiously consolidating themselves, not disintegrating their forces, not fatally weakening their sinews of war." These were the sombre phrases that sounded through the hushed air as the afternoon shadows deepened. The warning was pointed by deft references to the speeches of Mr. Churchill, and when Mr. Balfour had finished an ill-mirage had been conjured up—far more mesmeric than Lord Rosebery's carefully learnt-up nightmares—in which the United Kingdom, deeply severed by internal customs barriers, was seen wrestling simultaneously with foreign foes and an autonomous Ireland, an Ireland that had to be reconquered and her Parliament again destroyed by "blood and iron." "It was war with Spain," said Mr. Balfour, "that forced a union between England and Scotland. It was war with Napoleon that forced Ireland into that Union." [illegible] would it be, when all the resources of the Empire, including taxation, would be needed to resist aggression—taxation that might lose us Ireland as taxation once lost us the American colonies.

UNHAPPY CLIMAX.

It was to this unhappy climax that all Mr. Balfour's dialectic tended. Here was a supreme attempt to counter the universal approval of the British Dominions by argument, carefully purged of petty politics. The rest of the speech was of secondary importance. Mr. Balfour played all his usual cards—the Bill must be studied not only as it applied to Ireland but as it might hereafter be applied to England, Scotland, and Wales; it would take three years to pass, and after it other Home Rule Bills would follow, so making the congestion of useful legislation worse than ever; the Post Office was only wanted by the Nationalists for the sake of "patronage or bribery, which comes to the same thing"; who would give orders to the Royal Irish Constabulary, still to be paid for by Great Britain?—so ran the criticisms, many of which must await the text of the Bill. It was a preliminary survey of the vast field of obstruction which such a measure must offer to old Parliamentary hands, but it all converged on the question, "I admit that the Irishmen will be powerless at Westminster under the Bill. Yes; but will they be contented?"

Mr. Herbert Samuel quickly broke the spell woven about the imagination by these masterly incantations. Brisk and ruthless, he quoted yet again that unforgettable speech of doom in which Mr. Balfour wrote himself down to zero as a prophet of Empire by denouncing the grant of Home Rule to the Transvaal. "Who was right?" asked Mr. Samuel; yet I have always thought that on the other occasion it was in anger that Mr. Balfour spoke—anger at Mr. Churchill whom he did not love, and Sir Henry Campbell-Bannerman, whom he had not learnt to value. To-day Mr. Balfour was cool and sincere, but how completely out of touch with the British Dominions—yes, and with developments in Germany, where, as Mr. Samuel stated, an instalment of Home Rule has been granted to the border provinces of Alsace-Lorraine. As for the outcry against dealing step by step with devolution, what would Mr. Balfour have said if the Government had sought "constitutional tidiness" by going for the whole problem at once? There was no reason why every detail of Irish Home Rule should apply to England, Wales, and Scotland.

QUESTION OF FINANCE.

Turning to finance, Mr. Samuel added considerably to the Prime Minister's exposition. The Finance Commission had reported in favour of

> Complete fiscal autonomy for Ireland, including Customs and Excise.
>
> Exclusion of all Irish members from Westminster.
>
> A Treasury grant to Ireland of £900,000 annually.
>
> Existing pensions to be paid by Imperial Parliament, but new pensions to come on Irish Exchequer.

This provision as to pensions would have meant that in four years the grant of £900,000 would have been swallowed up; in 10 years the deficit would have

TO-DAY'S WEATHER.

London and Channel Forecast.—Light variable easterly breezes, becoming westerly to south-westerly later; fair or fine, local mist; temperature moderate to mild.

APRIL

16 MONDAY

17 TUESDAY

New Moon

18 WEDNESDAY

19 THURSDAY

20 FRIDAY

21 SATURDAY

Birthday of Queen Elizabeth II

22 SUNDAY

The Daily News, Tuesday, 16 April 1912: the sinking of the *Titanic*.

APRIL

23 MONDAY *St George's Day*

24 TUESDAY First Quarter

25 WEDNESDAY *Holiday, Australia and New Zealand (Anzac Day)*

26 THURSDAY

27 FRIDAY

28 SATURDAY

29 SUNDAY

The Daily Mirror, Friday, 27 April 1906: suffragettes demonstrate in the House of Commons.

The Daily Mirror

THE MORNING JOURNAL WITH THE SECOND LARGEST NET SALE.

776.   Registered at the G. P. O. as a Newspaper.   FRIDAY, APRIL 27, 1906.   One Halfpenny.

FFRAGETTES WHO RIOTED IN THE COMMONS AND WERE EXPELLED.

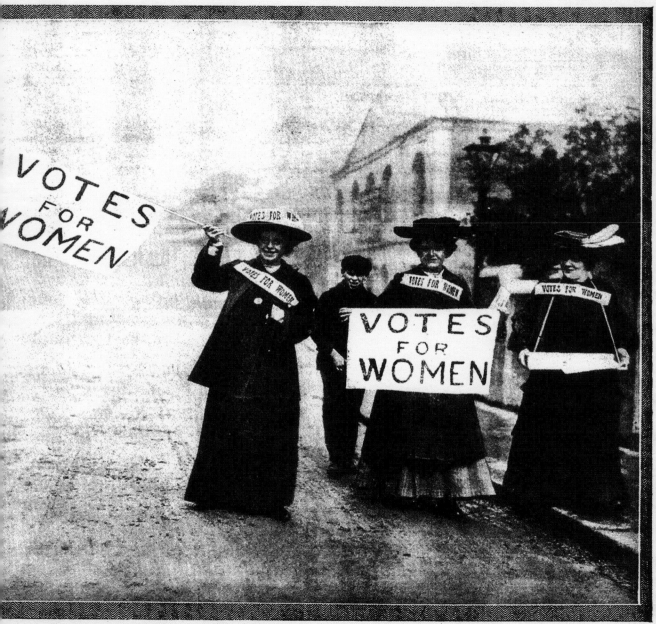

adies' Gallery at the House of Commons was the scene of a spirited disturbance dnesday night. When Mr. Evans was speaking on the motion for women's e, shrill cries of "Divide!" and "Justice for women!" re-echoed through the A white banner, bearing the words "Votes for Women," was thrust through the grille. Finally the Ladies' Gallery was cleared by the police. Reading from left to right, the photograph shows Miss Kenney, Miss Billington, and Mrs. Roe. The two former took an active part in the demonstration in the House, and were forcibly ejected.—(Specially taken by the *Daily Mirror*.)

We to
you fi

NINE days a
Sun said th
QE2 was
called up.
body deni
Yesterda
Ministry of
confirmed it.
really wa
know what's
on in the
The Sun. W
harder. See

GOTCHA

SUNK — AN Argie patrol boat like this one was sunk by missiles from Royal Navy helicopters after first opening fire on our lads

CRIPPLED — THE Argie cruiser General Belgrano . . . put out of action by Tigerfish torpedoes from our super nuclear sub Conqueror

Our lads sin gunboat and hole cruiser

From TONY SNOW aboard HMS Invincible

THE NAVY had the Argies on their knees last night after a devastating double punch.

WALLOP: They torpedoed the 14,000-ton Argentina cruiser General Belgrano and left it a useless wreck.

WALLOP: Task Force helicopters sank one Argentine patrol boat and severely damaged another.

The Belgrano, which survived the Pearl Harbour attack when it belonged to the U.S. Navy, had been asking for trouble all day.

The cruiser, second largest in the Argy fleet, had been skirting the 200-mile war zone that Britain has set up around the Falkland Islands.

MAJOR

With its 15 six-inch guns our Navy high command were certain that it would have played a major part in any battle to retain the Falklands.

But the Belgrano and

BATTLE FOR THE ISLAND

its 1,000 crew worry about the some time now.

For the nucle marine Conquere tained by Com Richard Wraith, with two torped

The ship w sunk and it is n how many cr there were.

HMS Conquer built at Cammell shipyard in Birk for £30million. S launched in 19

Continued on Pa

UNION BOYCOTTS WAR

A UNION chief is telling seamen on two ships taken over by the Government: "Don't go to war—the union can't protect you."

The astonishing advice comes from George Cartwright the Communist leader of the National Union of Seamen at Felixstowe Port in Suffolk.

The Government has just requisitioned the Townsend Thoresen roll-on, roll-off vessels Baltic Ferry and Nordic Ferry.

'Folly'

The ferries will carry troops and battle equipment in support of the QE2.

Mr Cartwright told the 150 seamen: "Our advice is that it would be folly to go off on a dangerous adventure.

"I'm old enough to remember that one in three merchant seamen were killed in the last war.

"It is not a case of being unpatriotic. We are not at war and our advice is based on union practicalities.

"What we are saying is that if seamen put themselves under military command, they will no longer have our protection.

Question

"There is no question of politics being behind the recommendation. We were asked for our view and gave our best advice."

He believes the majority of crew members will decide not to sail to the South Atlantic.

"So far I have heard from three seamen who want to go, the rest are non-committal or against joining the task force," Mr Cartwright said.

APRIL ~ MAY

30 MONDAY

1 TUESDAY

2 WEDNESDAY   Full Moon

3 THURSDAY

4 FRIDAY

5 SATURDAY

6 SUNDAY

The Sun, Tuesday, 4 May 1982: the British Navy torpedoes the Argentinian cruiser General Belgrano in the battle for the Falkland Islands.

MAY

7 MONDAY   *Early May Bank Holiday, UK and Republic of Ireland*

8 TUESDAY

9 WEDNESDAY

10 THURSDAY   Last Quarter

11 FRIDAY

12 SATURDAY

13 SUNDAY   *Mother's Day, Canada, USA, Australia and New Zealand*

Scottish Daily Express, Friday, 7 May 1954: Roger Bannister becomes the first man to
run the mile in under four minutes.

SCOTTISH
DAILY EXPRESS

No. 16,805 | Friday May 7 1954 | FOUNDED BY LORD BEAVERBROOK | Weather: Showers; bright periods | Price 1½d.

BANNISTER The mile 'shrinks' to 3mins. 59.4secs. **GENEVA** Molotov says to Eden: 'Let's get together' **BEVAN** 'Nonsense,' he shouts at Mr. Attlee **ESCAPE** Barlinnie man runs away in street

AT LAST—THE 4-minute MILE

THIS IS IT—THE DREAM OF ATHLETES COMES TRUE . . . BUT FIRST, SOME BREATH

BANNISTER DOES IT

British victory beats world

Express Staff Reporter

THE dream of world athletes through the years was achieved yesterday by a Briton—25-year-old Roger Bannister, who became the first man on earth to run a mile in under four minutes.

His feat at Oxford last evening—against a 25-mile-an-hour cross wind — was equal in dramatic achievement to the crashing of the sound barrier in the air.

Bannister's time officially recorded was **3MINS. 59.4SECS.** —beating the world record of Sweden's Gundar Haegg by 2secs.

Lap 1 : 57.5 secs.

It happened at the old university track—he is now a student at St. Mary's Hospital, Paddington—and 45 minutes before the attempt he had called it off.

It was to be Bannister's first race this season and the first attempt at the four-minute mile. And it was a cold damp evening. The flag of St. George flying on the nearby St. John's Church was fluttering in a stiff wind.

Bannister looked at the flag, looked at the sky — and went back to his dressing-room. "It would be stupid to try it to-day," he said.

Twenty-five minutes later he came out again. He looked up at the flag of St. George—the wind had dropped a bit. There was a double rainbow over the church.

Bannister said: "**RIGHT. I'LL TRY IT.**"

Lap 2 : 60.7 secs.

What was he trying? Experts had said it was impossible. Way back in 1886 Britain's Walter C. George had made the world gasp with a mile in 4min. 12.7secs.

After half - a - century of improved techniques, Britain's Sydney Wooderson clipped the time to 4mins. 6.4secs., and then in 1945 Gundar Haegg got it down to 4mins. 1.4secs.

For nine years those 1.4secs. had tantilised the world's athletes. Santee was trying hard in America, and Landy in Australia—and Bannister wanted to put Britain there first.

For the past three weeks he had been sitting examinations.

But "**RIGHT, I'LL TRY IT,**" he said at six o'clock last evening.

Lap 3 : 62.3 secs.

He lined up with Chris Chataway and Chris Brasher for the A.A.A. against Oxford University.

No tension. A couple of thousand people thinly lining the track. Straw-hatted boys lounging under golf umbrellas.

And then: **FIRST LAP**—57.5secs. **SECOND LAP**—1min. 58.2secs. **THIRD LAP**—3mins. 0.5secs.

Could he do it? The fourth lap in under 59.5secs.?

He didn't know then how fast he was running. But he ran the lap in 58.9secs.—and ran straight on into the almanacs of glory.

He finished fighting for breath, and as he broke the tape he fell headlong into waiting arms.

He was unconscious—and so the last man at the track to realise his success.

Lap 4 : 58.9 secs.

The crowd cheered and cheered. Bannister then murmured feebly: "Did I do it?"

He said last night: "This has been overrated. The important thing is to run against competitors, particularly against international competition—not against the clock."

But no such modest view was taken by his mother, who embraced him at the track—or his fellow-athletes.

Gordon Pirie, Britain's other hope, said in Bonn: "Gosh, that's fantastic! Can I beat it? I don't know. I'll have to wait and see and try."

Sydney Wooderson said: "It is absolutely wonderful. I always thought he would be the first to do it."

● Bannister, first man to beat the Four-Minute Mile, breaks the tape. . . . There was electricity along that side-line. . . . He was fighting for breath, his head rolling with fatigue — but his stride was superb.

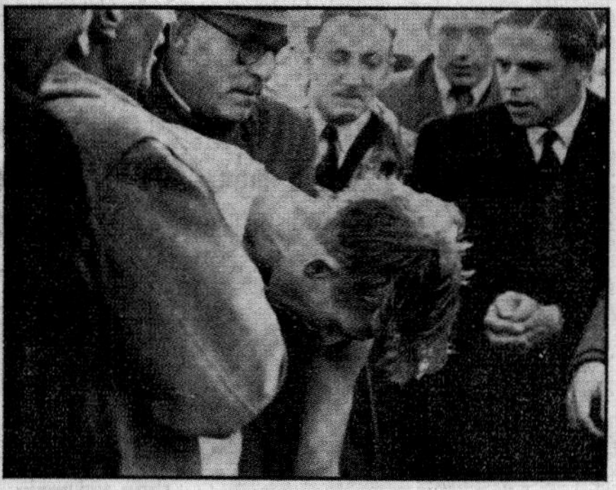

● A man clasps anxious hands. And Bannister, completely exhausted after his terrific effort, doubles up to regain breath.

YES, I MIGHT DO EVEN BETTER

By ROGER BANNISTER

—as told to a Daily Express reporter last night.

I HAVE never felt so good in all my life, and I am so glad it took a Briton to do this thing before America's Wes Santee and the other older chaps got down to it.

When I got into the last bend this evening I wasn't thinking anything in particular. I just couldn't think. I saw the tape faintly ahead, put everything into getting there and that was the last I knew about it.

You know, I think people have been frightened of this four-minute record. It has been rather like the sound barrier. Now it has been broken and I am sure other people will break it too.

I think in a way that the wind may have cut me down by two or three seconds and that I might make even better time in the future.

It was not until late today that I decided to try for the mile record because of the bad weather, but if you wait for the right weather in this country you wait a long time.

However, when I found I had broken the record I went off with friends to Vincent's Club at Oxford and had a pint of shandy.

Two peaks

Then I was rushed off to London and here I am. All I have had to eat since I ran the race is two sandwiches.

I think there could be a great race between Landy, of Australia, and Santee and myself.

Races against opponents do not tend to produce so fast a time because you are watching their tactics.

I am looking forward to doing well at the Empire Games at Vancouver this summer and at the games in Berne.

I have enjoyed every minute of running and it has given me wonderful opportunities for travelling. But I regard my medical career as more important.

Even today, if I considered the weather absolutely hopeless I would have waited to try another day. I feel that there are two peaks in my training this year.

One is the four-minute mile and then there are the Empire Games.

I don't really know if anybody would be interested if I reduced my time for the mile.

I would, in fact, be more interested in beating Santee alone than in achieving a faster time for the mile.

His problem

And slim, six-foot, fair-haired Roger Bannister said this to a TV audience from Lime Grove.

THE main problem was the weather. We were worried about the very strong winds, which might slow us down so much that we would not be able to run it under four minutes.

We set off with our plans fairly uncertain to run very hard and then, if the wind did not tire us too much, I was going to see if I could try and do it under four minutes.

I have been training with Brasher during the past three months.

Brasher set off and set the pace for the first half-mile. He reached the first lap in just under 59 seconds. In the third lap Chataway took over and reached the three-quarter mile in a shade over three minutes.

Tired

So I had to try and take over from them and do the last lap in about 59 seconds.

I was not really certain I was doing it and I was tired and it was not possible to assess the speed as accurately as you could earlier in the race.

I was particularly happy that the occasion should have been at Oxford where I had run my first mile ever in 1947, in the freshmen's when I was second.

I did a time of just over five minutes.

BIG in New York

Bannister was big news in the New York newspapers.

DID I DO IT?—HE GASPED

● Bannister, eyes closed, has a support-escort. He was the last to know he had made sports history.

● *In the duffel coat: Bannister's adviser, Franz Stampfl. On the right: George Truelove, A.A.A. team manager.*

A little party

Roger Bannister arrived at the Royal Court Theatre in London's Sloan-square as the audience was leaving last night. He strode through unrecognised and ran up a staircase to a club.

He was joined at a table by a tall, fair girl in an off-the-shoulder green gown. They sat talking and watching the dancing.

Here's his autograph, boys

6.00 p.m. EVENT 9. ONE MILE.
15. G. F. DOLE (Univ.)
16. A. D. GORDON (Magdalen)
58. T. N. MILLER (Univ.)
41. R. G. BANNISTER (Achilles)*
42. C. J. CHATAWAY (Achilles)*
1st 41 2nd 42 3rd 43 Time 3 59:4

One of the first things Roger Bannister did after his feat was to autograph a programme for Daily Express readers. . . . So cut it out, boys. It's history.

'Nonsense' shouts Bevan at leaders

Express Political Correspondent

MR. ANEURIN BEVAN shouted "Nonsense" last night when Socialist leaders gave reasons for postponing the "free-for-all" inquest on Mr. Morrison's attack on him.

Mr. Morrison — in a magazine article—has accused Mr. Bevan of losing seats for the party.

This personal attack caused many moderates in the party to demand an immediate meeting of all Socialist M.P.s to discuss Mr. Morrison's defiance of the rules.

Timing row

But last night the party leaders, who have agreed to such a meeting, got it postponed until May 19—*a day after* the executive meets.

The timing of the special meeting made the Bevanites angry because they believe the executive —*on the day before*—will issue orders to curb them.

Last night Mr. Attlee explained that such an idea had not occurred to him. He said the meeting could not be held next week because there was no suitable room available—and it would clash with other engagements.

This brought shouts of derision from the Bevanites. Afterwards one said: "There are 1,100 rooms in the Houses of Parliament—more than enough even for all our splinter groups."

£150 ring out car window

A woman threw a banana skin from her car yesterday—and lost a £150 diamond and emerald ring.

The ring fell from her finger to the roadside as she and her lawyer husband, Lieut.-Colonel G. W. Dunn, of Bloomfield, Arbroath, were driving towards Maidens, Ayrshire, on their way to Portpatrick for a holiday.

They searched for an hour with the village constable among thick grass and bracken but found nothing.

C.I.D. probe death

Detectives are investigating the death of a 24-year-old woman taken from a flat in Old Dumbarton-road, off Argyle - street, Glasgow, last night after an SOS for an ambulance. She died before reaching the Western Infirmary.

The strike-beater

VIENNA, Thursday. — Queen Frederika of Greece flew to Salzburg today. She hopes to settle a pay strike by farm workers on her nearby estates at Gruenau.—Express News Service.

BE FRIENDS, SAYS MOLOTOV

Talks with Eden go smoothly

From DEREK MARKS: Geneva, Thursday

A "LET'S-GET-TOGETHER" offer was made by Mr. Molotov to Mr. Eden at a dinner which the Foreign Secretary gave for the Soviet delegates to the Geneva Conference last night.

This morning, in accordance with Allied practice, Mr. Eden sent a report of what went on at the dinner to General Bedell Smith, leader of the U.S. delegation, and France's Foreign Minister M. Bidault.

Mr. Eden told them that Mr. Molotov was in his most friendly mood and had suggested it was much easier to deal with Britain than America.

Why, asked Mr. Molotov, did not Britain and Russia get together to settle outstanding world problems?

All sides rate the dinner as the most friendly which British and Russian diplomats have had since the war.

Mr. Eden and Mr. Molotov quickly reached decisions on procedure to be followed when talks

PAGE TWO, COL. FIVE

LATEST

THREE WARSHIPS SEEK PLANE

HALIFAX (Nova Scotia), Thursday.—Three warships sped tonight to a point off Halifax where a naval plane with four people aboard was believed to have crashed into the sea.—A.P.

Telephone: Bell 3550

Round-up (cont'd.)

CAIRO, Thursday.—Twenty more army officers, making a total of 45, have been arrested for "plotting."—A.P.

PRISONER ESCAPES

After a sixpenny bus ride to city

JOSEPH MEECHAN, 25-year-old Gorbals labourer serving a two-year sentence for theft in Barlinnie Prison, Glasgow, escaped yesterday after being taken on a sixpenny bus-ride to be X-rayed.

He was wearing his own dark grey suit, blue shirt and brown shoes.

A warder also in civilian clothes, escorted him on a No. 6 Corporation bus to the city's mass radiography unit in Elmbank-street.

When they left after an hour Meechan broke away in front of a tramcar.

The warder chased him to Waterloo-street. And there, near a post office, he disappeared.

Mrs. J. Marshall, an organiser at the radiography clinic, said last night: "The man was one of several Barlinnie prisoners taking part in a survey. It was his second visit."

A Scottish Office official said last night: "Prisoners always wear civilian clothes on such occasions. So do the prison officers. And public transport is always used."

DEPTFORD:
END OF AN
INQUEST
FULL STORY — PAGE 9

Exclusive Mail picture

POPE SHOT

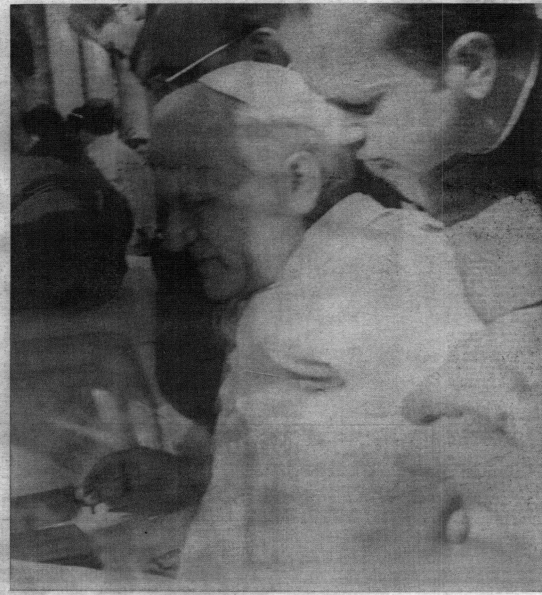

Blood stains his hand

THIS is the moment that stunned the world yesterday.

Pope John Paul II, shot by a Turkish fanatic already under sentence of death in Istanbul, staggers with blood dripping from his hand.

The scene in St Peter's Square, Rome, was captured in this exclusive Daily Mail picture.

Last night the Pontiff, four days away from his 61st birthday, was recovering from an emergency operation lasting four hours 20 minutes.

The operation was described as successful and doctors expect the Pope to make a complete recovery.

Consoling

Surgeon Dr Giancarlo Castiglioni said: 'He came through the surgery very well but we'll have to wait and see if any complications set in. He's now running a high fever.'

Cardinal William Wakefield Baum, Archbishop of Washington and a member of the Roman Curia, the Vatican Government, said: 'We have great hope. The reports we have heard are consoling. The news is favourable.'

The Pope was taken to the hospital's intensive care unit where he was expected to stay for up to 48 hours.

The Pope was wounded in five places, including the left hand, right arm and abdomen. Dr Castiglioni said he was not hit in any vital organs. At least one bullet passed right through his

Turn to Page Two, Col. 5

PICTURE: ALESSANDRO FOGGIA

MAY

14 MONDAY

15 TUESDAY

16 WEDNESDAY   New Moon

17 THURSDAY   *Ascension Day*

18 FRIDAY

19 SATURDAY

20 SUNDAY

Daily Mail, Thursday, 14 May 1981: an assassination attempt on Pope John Paul II in St Peter's Square, Rome.

MAY

21 MONDAY

---

22 TUESDAY

---

23 WEDNESDAY

Jewish Feast of Weeks (Shavuot)
First Quarter

---

24 THURSDAY

---

25 FRIDAY

---

26 SATURDAY

---

27 SUNDAY

Whit Sunday (Pentecost)

The Daily Mirror, Wednesday, 21 May 1913: a memorial to Captain Scott is erected in the Antarctic.

CAPTAIN SCOTT'S TOMB NEAR THE SOUTH POLE.

The Daily Mirror

24 Pages

THE MORNING JOURNAL WITH THE SECOND LARGEST NET SALE.

No. 2,987.   Registered at the G.P.O. as a Newspaper.   WEDNESDAY, MAY 21, 1913   One Halfpenny.

THE MOST WONDERFUL MONUMENT IN THE WORLD: CAPTAIN SCOTT'S SEPULCHRE ERECTED AMID ANTARCTIC WASTES.

It was within a mere eleven miles of One Ton camp, which would have meant safety to the Antarctic explorers, that the search party found the tent containing the bodies of Captain Scott, Dr. E. A. Wilson and Lieutenant H. R. Bowers. This is, perhaps, the most tragic note of the whole Antarctic disaster. Above is the cairn, surmounted with a cross, erected over the tent where the bodies were found. At the side are Captain Scott's skis planted upright in a small pile of frozen snow.—(Copyright in England. Droits de reproduction en France reservées.)

Daily Mail

SATURDAY, JUNE 1, 2002

60p

Queen Elizabeth II 1952-2002

LONG TO REIGN OVER US

MAY ~ JUNE

---

28 MONDAY

Spring Bank Holiday, UK
Holiday, USA (Memorial Day)

---

29 TUESDAY

---

30 WEDNESDAY

---

31 THURSDAY

---

1 FRIDAY

Full Moon

---

2 SATURDAY

---

3 SUNDAY

Trinity Sunday

Daily Mail, Saturday, 1 June 2002: the Queen's Golden Jubilee.

JUNE

---

4 MONDAY

Holiday, Republic of Ireland
Holiday, New Zealand (The Queen's birthday)

---

5 TUESDAY

---

6 WEDNESDAY

---

7 THURSDAY

Corpus Christi

---

8 FRIDAY

Last Quarter

---

9 SATURDAY

The Queen's official birthday (subject to confirmation)

---

10 SUNDAY

Daily Mirror, Tuesday, 6 June 1989: a student defies Chinese army tanks in a
peace protest in Tianenmen Square, Peking.

ONE MAN'S COURAGE THAT SAYS:

OUR FREEDOM

CANNOT DIE

THIS was one student's incredible act of defiance in Peking's Tiananmen Square yesterday.

Alone and unarmed, he boldly challenged the awesome might of the People's Army by standing in front of an advancing column of tanks.

It was a gesture that symbolised the courage of Chinese

● Turn to Page 2

CHINA CLOSE TO CIVIL WAR: Pages 2 and 3

Sunday Mirror
AND SUNDAY PICTORIAL

ENVOY IVANOV

The Profumo Scandal —LATEST

SOLICITOR EDDO

HP7

5d.   June 16, 1963 No. 11

WHAT CHRISTINE KEELER TOLD US

ABOUT THAT NUCLEAR QUESTIO

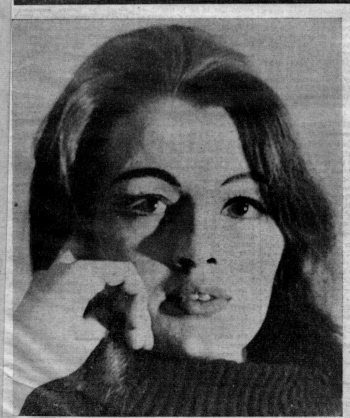

CHRISTINE KEELER, who has denied that the Russian diplomat Captain Eugene Ivanov asked her to obtain military information from the British War Minister, Mr. John Profumo, signed a statement that she was, in fact, asked to get information.

Not by Ivanov but by someone else.

Last February she signed articles she was proposing to sell to the Sunday Pictorial.

In the first of them she said:

❝ I did find it worrying when someone asked me to try to get from Profumo the answer to a certain question. That question was: "When, if ever, are the Americans going to give nuclear weapons to Germany?"

I am not prepared to say in public who asked me to find out the answer to that question. I am prepared to give it to the security officials. In fact, I believe now that ❝ I have a duty to do so. ❞

To Ronald Maxwell, the reporter who recorded the interview for her, she confided the name of the questioner.

Foolish

In view of the national importance which new developments have given to the story originally told to the Sunday Pictorial by Miss Keeler, copies of it were sent last night to the Prime Minister and to Lord Dilhorne, the Lord Chancellor, who has been inquiring into the security aspect of the Profumo Scandal.

In the story she told to the Sunday Pictorial, Miss Keeler also said that one man who was foolish enough and irresponsible enough to have an affair with her was a Minister, a Member of Her Majesty's Government. And at the same time she was having an affair with another man —a Russian diplomat.

If that Russian or anyone else had placed a

tape recorder or cine camera or both [in a] hidden place in her bedroom, said Mi[ss Keeler] it would have been very embarrassin[g for the] Minister, to say the least.

In fact, she said, it would have left [him open] to the worst possible kind of blackm[ail—the] blackmail of a spy.

Miss Keeler said she was not sugges[ting that] he really would have given up State [secrets to] avoid a scandal. He might have been [strong and] refused.

But she did believe that any man in [that posi]tion—particularly a married man—[who is] unwise and irresponsible to have an a[ffair with] some unknown girl like herself.

Miss Keeler said she was only eigh[teen. She] knew nothing of politics or internation[al affairs.] She was not interested.

She did not realise then that black[mail was] one of the Russians' favourite weap[ons when] they were trying to recruit traitors o[r steal] secret information.

'Harmless'

She said she was sure that Mr. Profu[mo would] not have allowed his "harmless" affai[r with her] to become a lever to prise secrets from [him.]

But she felt a weaker man in hi[s place] might have allowed it to happen.

At the time, however, she saw no [harm in] the situation. It just seemed funny t[hat] she should be seeing the two men, [Jack and Ivanov,] on the same day. One might leav[e her] only a few minutes before the other [arrived.]

In the second article Miss Keeler [describes her] contact between a third party and I[vanov. She] then wrote: "Jack stopped coming to [see me."]

The security question which Chri[stine was] asked to answer was not mentioned pub[licly until] Mr. Michael Eddowes, a London sol[icitor, an]nounced on Friday that he had writt[en to the] Prime Minister.

He wrote because he wanted to kno[w what] action had apparently been taken on [informa]tion which he had given to Scotla[nd Yard's] Special Branch on March 29.

In it he stated that when Miss K[eeler con]sulted him he asked if Ivanov and Pro[fumo were] friends of hers and she said: "Oh, ye[s."]

Mr. Eddowes said: "I asked if Iv[anov ever] asked her to get information. She sa[id: 'Yes.' I] said: 'Anything in particular?' Sh[e said:] 'The date of delivery of nuclear w[eapons to] Germany.' I asked her if she had t[aken any] information and she said: 'No.'"

The disclosure, made by Mr. Edd[owes at a] Press conference, was followed swi[ftly by a] denial, issued by the solicitors to [Miss] Keeler, that Ivanov had asked her [for any] information from Mr. Profumo.

But the statement did not deny th[at the nuclear] question had been asked by anyone e[lse.]

The Profumo Scandal—See al[so Pages] 2, 3 and Back.

CHRISTINE KEELER

Picture by Sunday Mirror Staff photographer Malcolm McNeill.

JUNE

11 MONDAY

Holiday, Australia (The Queen's birthday)

12 TUESDAY

13 WEDNESDAY

14 THURSDAY

15 FRIDAY

New Moon

16 SATURDAY

17 SUNDAY

Father's Day, UK, Canada and USA

Sunday Mirror and Sunday Pictorial, 16 June 1963: Christine Keeler, whose affair with John Profumo led to his resignation as Secretary of State for War, is interviewed by the national press.

JUNE

18 MONDAY

19 TUESDAY

20 WEDNESDAY

21 THURSDAY   *Summer Solstice*

22 FRIDAY   First Quarter

23 SATURDAY

24 SUNDAY

Daily Express, Tuesday, 19 June 1984: NUM president Arthur Scargill is injured during the miners' strike.

DAILY EXPRESS

Tuesday June 19 1984 ● 18p ● TV Pages 22 and 23   THE VOICE OF BRITAIN

IN THE
EAT NEW
VER CAR
— PAGE 26

Bloody Monday

100 days on... and Scargill is hurt as worst pit strike violence flares

■ **DAZED** and stumbling, miners' President Arthur Scargill clutches the baseball cap that has become a symbol of his campaign as he is helped by two riot ambulancemen on the most violent day of the pit strike.

■ This morning, the 100th of the dispute, he is in hospital, a victim of the war he started. Mr Scargill claimed he was hit by a police riot shield. Police said he tripped and knocked his head on a railway sleeper.

■ On the pit strike's Bloody Monday, 79 people were injured and 93 pickets arrested as bottles, bricks and iron bars became the weapons at the battle of Orgreave coking plant. "It is a miracle no one was killed," said a police chief.

THE BATTLE OF ORGREAVE: Pages 2, 3, 8 and centre pages

BARONET SENTENCED TO SIX MONTHS' IMPRISONMENT

Daily Mirror

TENNIS
ECLIPSES
AT WIMBLEDON

THE DAILY PICTURE NEWSPAPER WITH THE LARGEST NET SALE

No. 7,371 | Registered at the G.P.O. as a Newspaper | WEDNESDAY, JUNE 29, 1927 | One Penny

ENGLAND'S LAST TOTAL SUN ECLIPSE UNTIL 199

Crowds silhouetted against the radiance from the sun's corona during the eclipse at Westbury, Rhode Island, in 1925.

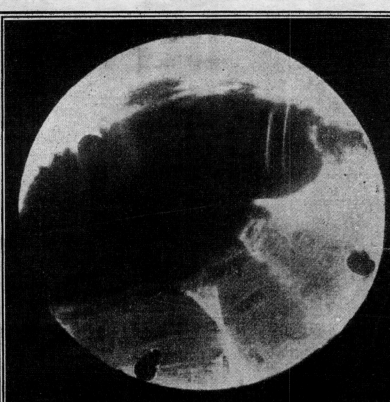

A radiograph of the sun specially obtained yesterday for *The Daily Mirror* by Mrs. Maud Dickinson at St. Albans, showing the radio-activity of the sun and earth eighteen hours before the eclipse. The light rings after fertilisation of the earth by the sun are clearly shown.

Nurses at a Lambeth hospital issued with tinted glasses for the eclipse.

Members of the Astronomer Royal's observation party examining coelostat at their camp at Giggleswick, Yorkshire.

Every route to the area from which the 23-second total eclipse of the sun might be seen this morning was yesterday taxed to its utmost, it being estimated that 500,000 people travelled northwards. The little market towns on the Yorkshire fells were crowded. The one anxiety was the weather, but pilgrims were heartened by the forecast that visibility would be mainly good, and that bright intervals were likely in most places. Londoners awaited with eager interest a partial view. See also pages 10 and 11.

JUNE ~ JULY

25 MONDAY

26 TUESDAY

27 WEDNESDAY

28 THURSDAY

29 FRIDAY

30 SATURDAY

Full Moon

1 SUNDAY

Daily Mirror, Wednesday, 29 June 1927: a total eclipse of the sun.

JULY

2 MONDAY   *Holiday, Canada (Canada Day)*

---

3 TUESDAY

---

4 WEDNESDAY   *Holiday, USA (Independence Day)*

---

5 THURSDAY

---

6 FRIDAY

---

7 SATURDAY   Last Quarter

---

8 SUNDAY

The Sun, Tuesday, 6 July 1999: the wedding of footballer David Beckham and Spice Girl Victoria Adams.

MR & MRS BECKS

THE FIRST PICTURE: *It's for real, folks! Soccer's David Beckham and pop queen Posh Spice sit on regal thrones at their fairytale wedding banquet — and you didn't have to wait for OK! magazine to see them*

ORE AMAZING WEDDING PHOTOS - Pages 2, 3, 4 & 5

Millions of people are worried about the fate of RUTH ELLIS. Today we ask our readers—

SHOULD HANGING BE STOPPED?

RUTH ELLIS . . . SHE WAS EXECUTED FOR MURDER OF HER LOVER. HER DEATH HAS THE WHOLE WORLD TALKI

YESTERDAY was not a happy day in Britain. The sun shone but the nation was upset.

At 9 a.m. in Holloway Gaol a woman of twenty-eight suffered death by hanging. Her body was later buried within the precincts of the prison.

Mrs. Ruth Ellis was not a virtuous woman. She admitted shooting one of her two lovers because she thought he was unfaithful. This was the gruesome end to a sordid affair.

Yet who in Britain yesterday felt happy that this mother of two children should lose her life —even though she herself had taken life?

Do the people of Britain believe that the punishment for murder should be CAPITAL PUNISHMENT?

M.P.s would not go past the prison

Are Members of Parliament satisfied that hanging is the expression of the public will?

Some M.P.s were NOT happy yesterday. Some who were to drive past Holloway Gaol on their way to the House of Commons took a different route to avoid the prison.

Five months ago M.P.s debated capital punishment. On a free vote they decided against a suggestion that the death penalty should be suspended FOR AN EXPERIMENTAL PERIOD OF FIVE YEARS and replaced by life imprisonment.

But did this vote mean that the majority of M.P.s were in favour of hanging? They voted against its suspension—not against its abolition.

One man had to decide her fate

How would they have voted on the straight question: Should we abolish the death penalty for good?

How would they vote today?

Because there is a death sentence, one man has a terrible responsibility. In court the witnesses give evidence, the jury return a verdict, the judge passes sentence. They all represent the public conscience. All did their duty at the trial of Ruth Ellis.

But one man—a professional politician who happens to be Home Secretary—had to decide whether this woman should be reprieved.

What an unenviable task.

While this young woman waited in her prison cell, one man had to decide whether there should be visited on her the retribution prescribed in a pitiless Biblical phrase:

" And thine eye shall not pity; but life shall go for life, eye for eye, tooth for tooth, hand for hand, foot for foot."

These words from the Old Testament Book of Deuteronomy were written probably 2,500 years ago, before the birth of Christ, by an unknown Jewish scribe.

And the enlightened British nation today still follows the teaching of all those centuries ago.

It is understandable why people in

Britain felt uneasy yesterday. In the rush of life the particular case of Ruth Ellis will be forgotten. But the problem of capital punishment remains.

Some murderers attract much public sympathy. There has been more talk about the fate of PRETTY YOUNG Ruth Ellis than there was about the similar fate of UGLY Mrs. Christofi, aged fifty-three, who strangled her daughter-in-law.

But is it unnatural if the execution of a pretty young mother causes public distress?

One fact remains:

Whether a murderess is pretty or ugly, Whether a murderer is young or old, Whether a killer attracts public sympathy or not—the lawful penalty is death by hanging.

Time for a change in the Law?

What the Ruth Ellis case has done is to focus attention on the whole problem of capital punishment.

People are asking:

Is hanging degrading to a civilised nation? Has the time come for hanging to be abolished in Britain?

—or—

Should hanging be retained as the just penalty for taking life?

The "Mirror" believes that the public should be able to voice its views.

Today we ask readers to give their verdict. There is a voting form in the Back Page.

● *The Last Hours of Ruth Ellis. — See Back Page.*

JULY

9 MONDAY

10 TUESDAY

11 WEDNESDAY

12 THURSDAY   *Holiday, Northern Ireland (Battle of the Boyne)*

13 FRIDAY

14 SATURDAY   New Moon

15 SUNDAY   *St Swithin's Day*

Daily Mirror, Thursday, 14 July 1955: Ruth Ellis becomes the last woman to be hanged for murder.

JULY

16 MONDAY

17 TUESDAY

18 WEDNESDAY

19 THURSDAY

20 FRIDAY

21 SATURDAY

22 SUNDAY   First Quarter

Evening Standard, Monday, 21 July 1969: the first landing on the moon.

Evening Standard

45,124   MONDAY, JULY 21, 1969   5d.

THE FIRST FOOTSTEP

Man's first footstep on the moon — a reconstruction of the historic moment.

Human footsteps crunch noiselessly on lunar soil—never to be erased for perhaps a million years.

One of two brave men gazes at this alien world through gold visors with almost unbelieving eyes. No wind, no rain, no sounds shatter the eerie silence. They are there!

Since time flowed, man has gazed at the moon and wondered. Neil Armstrong and Edwin Aldrin today are the first to touch it.

And, as TV screens glow 240,000 miles away, the watching earth pauses in its moment of destiny . . .

More moon colour on centre and back pages

Meet Louise, the world's first test-tube arrival
SUPERBABE

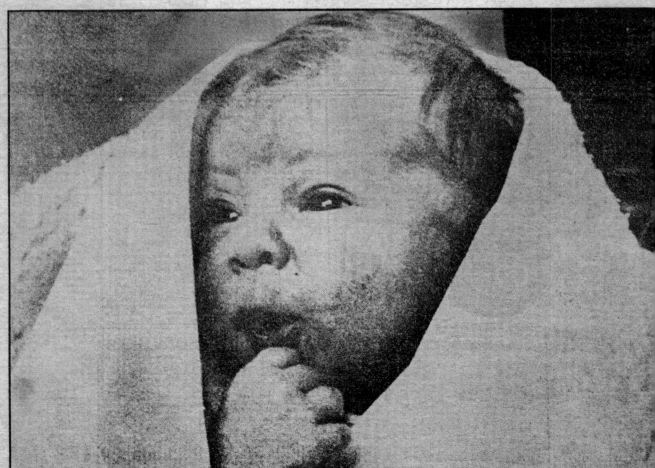

Wide-eyed Louise Brown pictured in hospital 18 hours after she was born. Today she's doing well. See Page Three

JULY

23 MONDAY

24 TUESDAY

25 WEDNESDAY

26 THURSDAY

27 FRIDAY

28 SATURDAY

29 SUNDAY

Evening News, Thursday, 27 July 1978: the world's first test-tube baby is born.

JULY ~ AUGUST

30 MONDAY   Full Moon

31 TUESDAY

1 WEDNESDAY

2 THURSDAY

3 FRIDAY

4 SATURDAY

5 SUNDAY   Last Quarter

News of the World, Sunday, 31 July 1910: Dr Hawley Harvey Crippen is arrested at sea for the murder of his wife.

NEWS OF THE WORLD.

SUNDAY EVENING EDITION

VOL. 136—No. 3,484 [Estab. 1843.]   LONDON, SUNDAY, JULY 31, 1910.   16 PAGES.   PRICE ONE PENNY.

CONTAINS MORE NEWS THAN ANY OTHER PAPER.

CRIPPEN'S LIFE AT SEA.

CAPTAIN KENDALL DESCRIBES HIS TERROR AND MISS LE NEVE'S MISERY.

THE HUNTED MAN WITH REVOLVER IN READINESS.

("News of the World" Special.)

Steadily the Montrose draws near to the consummation of one of the most dramatic scenes ever enacted on board ship. Within a few hours the Montrose will be off Father Point, Rimouski, and there Inspector Dew will come face to face with Hawley Harvey Crippen and Ethel Clara Le Neve. There famous masquerade will end for the masqueraders, and for their fellow-passengers, who will learn for the first time that the retired middle-aged man and his effeminate "son" stand in a very different relationship; that they are bound together by what would be called a more tender tie if it were not for the accusing spectre rising from the cellar of Hilldrop-crescent. By wireless messages from Captain H. G. Kendall, of the Montrose, an account has come to hand of the life of his notorious passengers. The man was nervous, ill-at-ease, the woman was all the time on the verge of hysterics. So abject was her terror that tears were seen in her eyes as she watched the man who had reduced her to such a condition. The man was desperate. Captain Kendall describes Crippen as having shaved off his moustache and altered his appearance in various ways. He passed himself off as a merchant, his "son" as a young student. But under the habiliments of the young student, the ship's officers soon discerned the figure and bearing, the talk and manners of a girl. Once the pair's disguise had been seen through, suspicion was, of course, aroused, and the identification of the pair was soon established. The result of careful observation, Capt. Kendall says the pair have no idea they have been discovered. The advent of the two officers will, therefore, come as a complete and staggering surprise. Meanwhile, Inspector Dew has landed at Father Point. There he awaits the coming of his quarry. The prisoners will be taken to safety, and may be either deported himself's as undesirable exiles, or extradited in the ordinary course.

WIRELESS MESSAGES.

GIRL'S LOVE BETRAYS.

CAPTAIN KENDALL TELLS HOW HE KNEW LE NEVE.

It was a love-passage between the runaway from Hilldrop-crescent and his female companion which first aroused Captain Kendall's suspicions. Standing on the bridge he saw the pair sitting apart sheltered by a boat. Some sign of endearment passed between the pair. It was only a kiss. But the shaved skipper knew that boys did not treat their fathers with such feminine tenderness. What followed on that incidental piece of observation is told in the following wireless message to the Montreal Star," No Central News, and latter from Captain Kendall.

SPECIAL TELEGRAMS.

Father Point (Quebec), July 30.

I have just received the following special wireless message from Captain Kendall, of the Montrose, despatched when the vessel was off Heath Point this morning:—

Off Heath Point, 7 a.m., July 30.

I feel quite convinced of the identity of the suspected pair, who booked at Antwerp, July 20. I have booked and his on. The man appears exactly to the description of Crippen as received from the police.

The "son" can also be easily identified as Miss Le Neve.

Captain Kendall is showing nervous nervousness in nearing land. He fears ap-

parently that he is suspected of being Crippen.

The girl is pale and worried-looking. The man spends sleepless nights.

Both keep in their room almost entirely.

All arrangements for effecting arrest have been made. We expect to reach Father Point early on Sunday.

We had only been at sea a couple of hours when

MY SUSPICIONS WERE AROUSED

as to the younger passenger's disguise. The "son" was observed to treat the "father" with extraordinary signs of endearment.

This was so unusual as between men as to excite suspicion.

Montreal, July 30.

The Montreal "Star," in a further lengthy wireless message from Captn Kendall, of the Montrose, gives other interesting details. He says:—

Crippen came on deck early this morning while we were passing Belle Isle.

He was looking worried, and continued pacing the deck about two hours.

Le Neve seems very depressed, and even tearful. She kept her room practically all day yesterday.

There is no proof that either Crippen or Le Neve suspects they are being watched.

Crippen complains of insomnia, and looks very haggard.

When the couple were lunching the first day out their hats were hanging up outside the dining saloon, and I noticed that the "boy's" was several sizes too large.

Later I saw Le Neve with coat and waistcoat off, and I noticed that the trousers were attached at the waist by means of a safety-pin. Crippen carries a revolver; surely a suspicious circumstance.—Central News.

Father Point, July 30 (Later).

The wireless telegraph operator on board the Montrose telegraphed at seven o'clock this morning, when the ship was abreast of Health Point:

Crippen and Le Neve have become more retiring than ever.

The couple have not been arrested, and they still have no suspicions of the observation that was being kept on them.—Reuter.

CANNOT BE PARTED.

CRIPPEN AND MISS LE NEVE INSEPARABLE ON SHIP.

The world-wide curiosity as to whether Crippen was really aboard the Montrose was earlier satisfied with the following despatch from Captain Kendall:—

"Doctor Crippen wanted London for murder of Belle Elmore, actress, aboard."—Reuter.

A further wireless account despatched from Point Amour, amplified this to the extent of stating that Miss Le Neve was also on board, and that their identity had been established "beyond all doubt." Following up this came the captain's account of the disguise which had been adopted by Crippen, as follows:—

Montreal, July 29.—Captain Kendall, of the Montrose, has supplied by wireless extensively to the "Montreal Star" the following very interesting statement regarding his two passengers, in whom so much interest is taken:—

I am confident they are Crippen and Le Neve. The man continues to shave his upper lip, and is growing a beard.

Crippen has no suspicion his identity is suspected, and the passengers also are ignorant of the remarkable situation in which they are unconsciously acting a part.

Le Neve refrains from talking. They have no baggage with them.

At times they have appeared to be labouring under anxiety, and have conversed together in subdued tones during the night hours.

From this it has been remarked that Crippen and his companion have been obtaining but little sleep.

Miss Le Neve is dressed in a grey suit, and when on deck wears a brown hat.

Not only has Crippen's moustache gone and a fortnight's growth of beard appeared, but prominent eyebrows are displaced. His elaborate waistcoats have been replaced by a soberer kind, more befitting the dress of a merchant.

Crippen explains his occasionally worried expression of face by telling the solicitous passengers that he is anxious about the son's breakdown—caused by overwork at his studies.

At times Miss Le Neve was observed to be watching Crippen with tearful eyes.—

A TOUCHING PROPOSITION.

Already Inspector Dew is proving himself a "tough proposition" to the American and Canadian reporters, who are used to the less reserved methods of their own police. The special correspondent of the Central News at Father Point says Inspector Dew "has brought the silence, as well as the science, of Scotland Yard with him, and his manner towards pressmen is decidedly frosty. Two correspondents secured rooms in the hotel where he is staying, but no sooner did the fact become known to Mr. Dew than he went to the proprietor, and announced that if they remained there he should depart elsewhere. The pressmen went. Mr. Dew last night paid visits to the Marconi and telegraph stations."

CRIPPEN COMPLAINS OF INSOMNIA.

SLEEPLESS NIGHTS.

HUNTED MAN UNABLE TO OBTAIN RESPITE FROM FEAR.

Later came the following:—

New York, July 29.—Another wireless message has been received from Captain Kendall, of the Montrose, in which he says:

During the voyage Crippen showed unmistakeable signs of extreme nervousness. Miss Le Neve was alternately gay and sad.

One of the most noticeable traits in the dispositions of Crippen and Miss Le Neve has been their obvious disinclination to mingle with the other passengers.

COURSE OF ACTION.

PROBABLE EXCLUSION OF THE DOCTOR AS AN "UNDESIRABLE" IMMIGRANT.

Rimouski, July 30.—At seven o'clock this morning the Montrose was reported off East Point, 250 miles distant. This should mean her arrival at Father Point at five o'clock to-morrow (Sunday) morning, if not sooner at Greenwich.

As some doubt exists as to the legal position of Dr. Crippen and Miss Le Neve, the opinion was obtained to-day of Judge Chauveau. He expressed the belief that, in view of the circumstances of the case, the procedure to be adopted will be that

TO THE MONTROSE.

HAND OF THE LAW ON MAN FROM HILLDROP-CRESCENT.

At 8 a.m. the Montrose had hove in sight. Fifteen minutes later the beginning of the end had come, so far as Crippen's flight was concerned.

Father Point, July 31, 8.15 a.m.—The tender has left to meet the Montrose, which has hove sighted in the Gulf. The weather is very foggy.—Reuter.

ON THE WAY TO QUEBEC.

FIRST STAGE IN TRIAL OF CRIPPEN FOR HIS LIFE.

Following upon this message came the wireless telegram stating that the deed was done; that "Robinson's" nervousness was fully justified by his real character. Inspector Dew at once identified the "merchant" from Antwerp as Dr. Hawley Harvey Crippen, "the man wanted," and his companion as the typist, Miss Le Neve, and the Canadian officers at once acted upon the warrants in their possession. Inspector Dew at four o'clock this afternoon received official intimation from Chief Inspector Dew that :

"Crippen and Le Neve had been identified and arrested;"

"And that they were now on their way to Quebec."

CRIPPEN AND WIRELESS ROMANCE.

A scientific interest attaches to the arrests. The long arm of the law has been lengthened by the Marconigram, and the captures now effected will long be remembered in connection with the development of wireless telegraphy.

(Continued on page 2.)

THE ORDER OF RELEASE.

With acknowledgments to the picture by Sir John Millais, P.R.A.

The couple cannot be parted, and are very reticent.

The man has evidently travelled much. He is generally busy reading books, and appears to be very sleepless.

The first clue as to the identity of the couple was obtained two hours after we left Antwerp.

The man says he is taking the boy to California for his health. He spends much of his time in his room.

Mr. LLEWELLYN JONES, THE MARCONI OPERATOR.

Careful watch was in consequence kept, and suspicion was strengthened that young Robinson was a girl.

The clues were numerous. The "boy's" attire was ill-fitting, revealing a figure of feminine proportions.

The hands and feet were those of a woman.

I spoke with the supposed boy. The voice and demeanour convinced me that Master Robinson was playing a part.

Crippen was ill at ease. He did not wish the companion to speak apart. Nor did she desire to make acquaintances. Our observations were made as guardedly and rationally that, even after we had discovered everything, Crippen was satisfied with his disguise.

During their absence from their state-room their belongings were inspected. They had kept to no luggage.

The woman's belongings left scarcely a doubt as to her sex. During meal time these were examined at leisure.

When suspicion had become certainty watch was kept night and day.

Throughout the night the couple lay awake, speaking in subdued voices.

In the morning Crippen looked haggard and wretched. The girl kept to her cabin as much as possible.

When spoken to about the wretched looks as he paced the deck, Crippen complained that

HIS BOY'S HEALTH

troubled him.

As the Montrose drew nearer land the nervousness increased.

The boy appears bright at times, but shows signs of worry. The man looked as a merchant; the boy as a student.—Central News.

FLANS FOR ARREST.

DETECTIVES IN DISGUISE.

SURPRISES IN STORE FOR THE UNSUSPECTING FUGITIVE.

When the Montrose reaches Father Point to-day the passengers who will watch the approach of the Customs' boat with the greatest interest will be Crippen, with his "son" at his side. As stated by Captain Kendall, he is in complete ignorance of all that has happened in the last ten days, and in the happy delusion that no one has recognised him or his companion on the Montrose, he will be anxious to get hold of a newspaper to learn, if possible, if he has succeeded in throwing the police off the scent. Cool, clever, and resourceful though he is, the "Dr." would be more than flesh and blood if he were not anxious as to the result of this first communication with land since July 20. He will suffer more than a slight uneasiness at the thought that the information of his flight from Antwerp has been flashed across the ocean, either by cable or wireless, while the Montrose has been slowly making her way to the Gulf of St. Lawrence. As he leans over the side of the vessel among the other passengers he will, therefore, be keenly on the look-out for any sign of danger to himself in the visit of the Customs boat. The sight of a police uniform would instantly startle him into fears for his safety, and he has, we know, a revolver in his pocket. Crippen will, however, see no police in uniform when the boat swings round to the side of the Montrose. He will see the Customs officers and one or two assistants in their usual innocent garb. Among these assistants will be a couple of Canadian police officers and Inspector Dew who, as stated, landed on Friday. The Laurentio, in which he made the voyage, having easily outdistanced the Montrose. Mr. Dew will be so disguised that his own mother would not recognise him. He will take care, also, not to force himself on the attention of Crippen till the proper moment. Arrangements have been made with Captain Kendall as to the manner in which the position of Crippen and his companion will be pointed out when once the police are on board. The captain will be careful not to lose sight of the suspects when the Montrose comes to anchor, and he will be able to indicate at once where they are. Inspector Dew will choose an opportunity of identifying Crippen without arousing himself too prominently, and if given to the Canadian police the signal that he is the man wanted, the arrest will be made at once. From the moment Crippen is arrested until Quebec is reached, he will be watched night and day by police officers, lest he should attempt suicide. The authorisation given to Detective Inspector of the Canadian police, who will be actually in charge of the fugitives on their return to England, gives them the primary to organise cabins, and make certain that man chance is given either of committing suicide.

Inspector Dew will give such information as will enable the immigration authorities to reject Dr. Crippen on his arrival in Quebec as an "undesirable."

This course obtains the possibility of legal complications, are immediately upon the order for their deportation being made, the two prisoners can be placed in charge of Inspector Dew for return to England by the next steamer.

In the course of conversation last night Inspector Dew mentioned his interview with Dr. Crippen on the day before the latter's disappearance, and recalled how in reply to the enquiry where Mrs. Crippen had been removed, Dr. Crippen replied that owing to trouble with his wife about some other woman, she had taken her departure for California, whence also intended to quit some of her friends.

The local detectives who have been detailed to assist Inspector Dew in the arrest state that they have every reason to believe

ALIEN'S SECRET HOARD.

An inquest has been held on the body of a Roumanian named Maurice Gold, 60, who was found dead in bed at his lodgings in Sixteen-st., St. Pancras. Medical evidence showed death to be due to heart failure while suffering from bronchitis and heart disease. A constable stated that in an old bag under the man's bed were found five £5 Bank of England notes, one French note for 50fr. francs, and a Post Office bank book showing £84 balance.—Mr. Schroder stated that many people preferred to keep their money uninvested, thinking that it afforded greater security.

INSP. DEW'S RECEPTION.

THE FIRST PASSENGER TO LAND AT FATHER POINT FOR MANY YEARS.

The following cable was received from Reuter's correspondent at Father Point yesterday, describing the arrival of Inspector Dew:—

At half-past three, a cloud of smoke on the eastern horizon betokened the approach of the Laurentic. All was astir in the quaint of summer visitors, and the home of priests.

The Government tug Eureka was almost uncomfortably crowded with newspaper men, artists, and other privileged persons. The Laurentic hoved high above the little tug, and her sides were lined with passengers, evidently curious to know the reason of the invasion from the shore.

Among those on board the Eureka was the inspecting medical officer of the Immigration Department, who was specially commissioned to board the Laurentic here, in order to enable Inspector Dew to land.

The regulations are that no passenger shall be allowed to go on shore from incoming steamers until their arrival at the quarantine station at Grosse Isle.

The doctor had not been many minutes on the Laurentic when Inspector Dew came

down the gangway wearing a heavy tweed overcoat and a cloth cap.

He found himself the centre of attraction on the tug, and he took for quite a battery of cameras.

The pressmen crowded round the inspector to interview him, but he would only say that he had nothing to communicate.

On landing Inspector Dew was driven to the house of Chief Constable McCarthy, where he will remain until the arrival of the Montrose, which, it is now stated, will get in this morning.

The Laurentic will be detained, at Grosse Isle, on account of the outbreak of measles on board reported by the ship's physician.

Inspector Dew, according to the correspondent, is the first passenger to land at Father Point for many years.

Miss LE NEVE AS SHE NOW APPEARS.

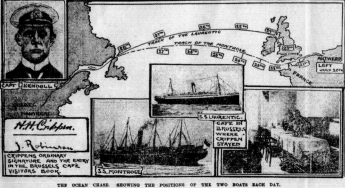

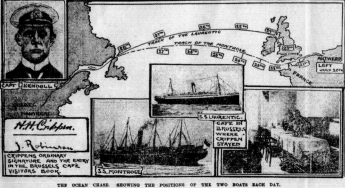

Crippens ordinary signature and the entry in the Brussels café visitors book.

S.S. MONTROSE.

CAPT. KENDALL.

ANTWERP LEFT JULY 20TH

TRACK OF THE MONTROSE

TRACK OF THE LAURENTIC

THE OCEAN CHASE. SHOWING THE POSITIONS OF THE TWO BOATS EACH DAY.

STOP PRESS

CRIPPEN ARRESTED.

DRAMATIC SCENE ABOARD THE MONTROSE.

FUGITIVES TAKEN INTO CUSTODY AT END OF VOYAGE.

Father Point (Rimouski), July 31.—Crippen and Le Neve have both been identified and arrested.—Reuter.

INSPECTOR DEW BOARDS LINER.

Father Point, July 31.

By special arrangement Inspector Dew this morning boarded the steamer Montrose from a coving boat leaving the numerous newspaper correspondents to follow in the Government tender Eureka.

The object of this proceeding was to enable the detective to make the arrest without previously arousing the suspicions of "Dr." Crippen and Miss Le Neve.—Reuter.

Mr. Dew was disguised as a pilot.—Central News.

FINAL PLANS FOR ARREST.

HOOTS FROM LINER SIGNAL CRIPPEN'S SEIZURE.

Earlier came tidings of the plans finally made for the arrest as follows:—

Father Point, July 31.

After eight hours' interruption, indirect communication with the Montrose via Fame Point and Clark City was restored at eight o'clock this evening.

At 12.30, when the Montrose was 70 miles east of Fame Point, Captain Kendall telegraphed that the position was unchanged.

Later he informed Inspector Dew that the suspects were becoming increasingly nervous.

Late last night Inspector Dew informed the pressmen that, owing to the necessity for the absence of any time in connection with the identification of the suspects, he and the Canadian police would put out in a small boat as soon as the Montrose arrived.

When the police had completed their business, the vessel would give two hoots as a signal that the tender might bring the pressmen aboard.—Central News.

EMERGED FROM FOG.

WATCHERS IN EARLY HOURS DESCRY MONTROSE APPROACH.

Another message describes the long and weary vigil kept ashore by the army of policemen and pressmen, and now the liner at length loomed in sight, emerging from the fog that had hung over the great river.

Father Point, July 31, 8 a.m.—The dense fog which set in at half past eleven last night began to lift at a quarter to eight this morning. Above the roar of the Father Point foghorn was heard a steamer's whistle, and the watchers on the shore took this as an indication of the proximity of the Montrose. If the fog continues to lift, it is expected that the vessel will be off Father Point soon after eight o'clock.—Reuter.

THE Sun

Monday, August 11, 2003   30p   www.thesun.co.uk

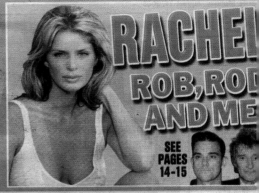

RACHEL ROB, ROD AND ME

SEE PAGES 14-15

Love cheat . . . Best yesterday

Bestie's missus leaves in tears

EXCLUSIVE by JOHN ASKILL

THE cheated wife of soccer legend George Best wept yesterday and said: "I am devastated."

Alex, 31, flew back to Britain alone from their holiday in Malta after it was revealed Best had been dating blonde Paula Shapland, 25.

Distraught Alex burst into tears at Gatwick airport and said: "I can't believe he would do this — would be so naive.

"I don't know what will happen to us now."

But pals revealed Alex, who nursed Best, 57, through alcoholism and a life-saving liver transplant, had confided she was **RELIEVED** her troubled marriage was over.

She told them: "I'm so hurt. I can't stop crying.

"Yet I'm glad it's over. I couldn't put up with it any longer. I've wanted to walk out for weeks."

Full Story — Page Seven

Torment . . . Alex at Gatwick

101° HOTTEST DAY IN HISTORY

By MICHAEL LEA

BRITAIN had its hottest ever yesterday — as temperature soared to 101°

The record-breaking h (38.1°C) was at Gravesend, Ken

The Met Office said: "We're stunne

It was a sizzling day across South England. Five places beat the UK's pr ous highest temperature of 98. recorded in Cheltenham, Gloucs, in 19

But there were floods as storms Yorkshire, Teesside, and the North W

Full Story — Pages Four, Five & Six

Swell-tering . . Sussex beach yester

Atkins Diet: TRUTH ABOUT A SLIMMING SENSATION

AUGUST

6 MONDAY   *Summer Bank Holiday, Scotland and Republic of Ireland*

7 TUESDAY

8 WEDNESDAY

9 THURSDAY

10 FRIDAY

11 SATURDAY

12 SUNDAY   New Moon

The Sun, Monday, 11 August 2003: Britain's hottest day on record.

AUGUST

---

13 MONDAY

---

14 TUESDAY

---

15 WEDNESDAY

---

16 THURSDAY

---

17 FRIDAY

---

18 SATURDAY

---

19 SUNDAY

The Sun, Wednesday, 17 August 1977: the death of rock 'n' roll king Elvis Presley.

HE WAS 42 AND ALONE

KING ELVIS DEAD

From ROSS WABY   in New York

ELVIS PRESLEY, the rock 'n' roll king who thrilled millions, died alone yesterday aged 42.

He was felled by a massive heart attack . . . and died in his mansion home before help could reach him.

Elvis, who had been ill for some time, was found by his road manager Joe Esposito.

Mr Esposito sent for an ambulance and tried to revive Elvis.

Then medical staff massaged the superstar's heart as the ambulance sped from his home in Memphis, Tennessee to the city's Baptist hospital.

FATHER

Elvis's personal doctor, George Nichopoulos, who was in the ambulance, kept imploring the singer: "Come on, Presley, breathe. Breathe for me."

Doctors then battled for half an hour before announcing that he was dead.

Dr Nichopoulos said later that he suspected a h e a r t attack was the cause of death, but this could not be confirmed until a post mortem examination.

Big crowds gathered outside the hospital, where Elvis's 61-year-old father, Vernon, went with other relatives after death was confirmed.

"I don't know why we are here— we're just paying our condolences," said a middle-aged woman who stood with a throng at the hospital gates.

The sudden death will shock millions of Elvis fans world-wide.

But it was no surprise to those close to him.

For Elvis, the poor boy who became the world's highest paid performer, was the victim of his own phenominal success.

His millions enabled him to indulge his every whim, and that led to his undoing and his death.

His fondness for junk food—hamburgers and soft drinks—became an addiction, as did his thirst for thrills and experiences . . . and drugs.

Elvis sought kicks with cars, motorcycles, women, p a r t i e s, guns, pinball machines, pool tables and no timetable.

He liked to stay up late —all night if he was enjoying himself—surrounded by the cousins and bodyguards that comprised his "Memphis Mafia."

DRUGS

To keep his body going as he sated himself, he turned more and more to drugs.

Red West, a bodyguard, said recently: "He takes pills to go to sleep, he takes pills to get up, he takes pills to go to the lavatory, and he takes pills to stop him from going."

West, sacked last year, after a row with his boss and boyhood friend, re vealed the extent of Elvis's drug taking.

"He was a walking pharmaceutical shop. He takes uppers and downers and all sorts of very strong painkillers—perco—

Continued on Page Two

A massive heart attack at mansion

The idol who had the whole world rocking
Pages 4 and 5

D FORTY . . . One of the last pictures of rocking king Elvis Presley on stage in America His overeating made him a tragic sight

CHESS BIDS TO HALT TV SERIES—Page 2

NO RIND.....
.....NO WASTE
CHEDLET
CHEESE
Aplin & Barrett & The Western Counties Creameries, Ltd.

News Chronicle
POSTAGE: in U.K., 1d.; Canada, 1d.; Abroad, 1½d.
No. 26,632 LONDON WEDNESDAY, AUGUST 26, 1931 MANCHESTER ONE PENNY

Holbrook's
Worcestershire SAUCE
A mere suggestion helps digestion

NATIONAL CABINET OF TEN

Four Labour, Four Conservatives and Two Liberals

SIR HERBERT SAMUEL (Home Secretary).

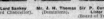

Lord Reading (Foreign Secretary). Sir Samuel Hoare (India). Mr. N. Chamberlain (Health). Mr. Baldwin (Lord President of the Council).

Mr. Ramsay MacDonald leaving No. 10 by the garden door to submit the names of the Cabinet to the King.

Mr. Snowden (Chancellor of the Exchequer). Lord Sankey (Lord Chancellor). Mr. J. H. Thomas (Dominions). Sir P. Cunliffe-Lister (Board of Trade).

£100,000,000 IF WE WANT IT

AMERICA EAGER TO HELP BRITAIN

NEW GOVERNMENT HAILED

From Our Own Correspondent

NEW YORK, Tuesday.

LEADING bankers here, who have expressed their willingness to extend virtually unlimited credit to the National Government in support of sterling, would not be surprised if an international loan of £100,000,000 is eventually floated.

American and French bankers would, of course, furnish the bulk of the loan. This speculation has no basis in any request from London and simply reflects Wall Street opinion, but it is significant as showing the depth of confidence felt in the new Government's ability to handle the situation.

Not in London itself could implicit trust in the National Administration be stronger. Indeed, there is a tendency in some financial circles to chide London for painting the financial picture in darker colours than are justified.

ADMIRATION FOR PREMIER

Both Wall Street and newspapers hail the creation of the Government as a great constructive act, and admiration is expressed for the courageous patriotism and political courage of Mr. MacDonald in jeopardising his career for the sake of his country.

If credit is asked it will be given eagerly in the present mood of America. It is likely to be an arrangement between the British Government and private bankers, because the Federal Reserve is not allowed by law to extend credit to foreign Governments, its previous accommodations having been extended to the Bank of England.

Six years ago the British Treasury obtained £20,000,000 credit, which, incidentally, was not used, from a group of Wall Street banks headed by Morgan's. This operation, then necessitated by the return to the gold standard, is likely to be taken as a precedent for dealing with the present situation.

HOOVER PLEASED

Washington also has expressed its faith in the new Government and its admiration for the resolve of the British party leaders to balance the Budget.

President Hoover discussed the situation in all its bearing to-day with Mr. Mellon and was particularly happy to learn that the change of Government would not affect the great scheme of disarmament on which he has set his heart.

CITY REASSURED

CHEERING NEWS FROM ABROAD

From Our City Editor

Bankers found yesterday that the proposed formation of a Government of Co-operation to "correct without delay the excess of national expenditure over revenue" and to submit plans "for a very large reduction in expenditure" had an immediately reassuring effect abroad, as revealed in messages from foreign customers and depositors.

This improved sentiment had its reflex in improved prices for Government securities. Rises were from 2s. 6d. to 7s. 6d. Industrial shares also were moderately higher. Though City tension has been relieved, it has not turned to exuberance.

The composition of the new Cabinet was announced after City hours, but the absence of heads of spending departments from its members and its inference of rigid economies will be to the taste of financial authorities closely in touch with overseas interests.

LORD READING AS NEW FOREIGN SECRETARY

SIR AUSTEN AS FIRST LORD WITHOUT SEAT IN CABINET

MR. BALDWIN TO LEAD THE HOUSE

After a day of interviews Mr. MacDonald went to Buckingham Palace last evening and submitted his list of new Ministers for the approval of his Majesty. The list was issued later as follows:

THE NATIONAL CABINET

Mr. J. RAMSAY MACDONALD	Prime Minister and First Lord of the Treasury.
Mr. STANLEY BALDWIN	Lord President of the Council (Leader of the House).
Mr. PHILIP SNOWDEN	Chancellor of the Exchequer.
Sir H. SAMUEL	Home Secretary.
LORD SANKEY	Lord Chancellor.
LORD READING	Foreign Secretary.
Sir SAMUEL HOARE	Secretary for India.
Mr. J. H. THOMAS	Secretary for the Dominions and Colonies.
Mr. N. CHAMBERLAIN	Minister of Health.
Sir P. CUNLIFFE-LISTER	President of the Board of Trade.

NOT IN THE CABINET

LORD AMULREE	Secretary for Air.
Sir A. CHAMBERLAIN	First Lord of the Admiralty.
Sir A. SINCLAIR	Secretary for Scotland.
Sir D. MACLEAN	President of the Board of Education.
Sir H. BETTERTON	Minister of Labour.
LORD LONDONDERRY	First Commissioner of Works.
LORD LOTHIAN	Chancellor of the Duchy of Lancaster.
Sir JOHN GILMOUR	Minister of Agriculture.
The Secretary of War is	to be announced later.

PREMIER'S BROADCAST

CRISIS 'NOT BANKER'S RAMP': DOLE TO BE CUT

IN a speech broadcast last night from No. 10, Downing-street, through all B.B.C. transmitters, Mr. Ramsay MacDonald said:

I speak to-night under unusual and to me rather sorrowful circumstances. I have given my life to the building up of a political party.

I was present at its birth. I was its nurse when it emerged from its infancy and had attained adult years.

At this moment I have changed none of my beliefs and none of my ideals.

I see that it is said that I have no Labour credentials for what I am doing. That is true. I do not claim to have them, though I am certain that in the interests of the working classes I ought to have them.

Be that as it may I have credentials of even higher authority. My credentials are those of national duty as I conceive it, and I obey them irrespective of consequences.

You will have read in the daily papers during the last few weeks of great activity in London. For my

CONTINUED ON PAGE 2, COL. 2.

INDIA CONFERENCE

NO CHANGE IN THE ARRANGEMENTS

It was announced last night from No. 10, Downing-street, that arrangements made for the India Round Table Conference would not be affected by the change of Government.

The Prime Minister will be chairman. Lord Sankey will preside at the forthcoming meeting of the Federal Structure Committee, and Lord Reading will continue to lend assistance in its work.

GANDHI MAY COME

TO-DAY'S TALK WITH VICEROY

SIMLA, Tuesday.

It is now definitely anticipated in Congress circles that Mr. Gandhi will attend the Round Table Conference in London, and he is expected to sail either on Saturday this week or by next week's boat.

He will meet the Viceroy (Lord Willingdon) at 11 o'clock to-morrow morning.

To-day Mr. Gandhi had a long conversation with Mr. Emerson, the Home Secretary, regarding alleged breaches of the Delhi Pact, particularly in Gujerat, where it is understood that an inquiry will probably be held.

The Viceroy, who is recovering from his indisposition, had a meeting with the Executive Council to-day.—Reuter.

NO GAS IN JERSEY

NEARLY 4-INCHES OF RAIN IN 24 HOURS

The greater part of Jersey was in darkness last night, owing to the flooding of the gasworks which supply St. Helier and most of the island.

During 24 hours the rainfall was no less than 3.77 inches, an amount without precedent in Jersey.

In the retort house of the gasworks water was 4ft. to 5ft. deep, and the fire brigade worked all last night trying to pump out the flooded area.

Boarding houses full of visitors are finding it difficult to prepare meals without gas.

SIX LIVES LOST IN GALE

TRAWLER ABANDONED

LA ROCHELLE (France), Tuesday.

Six of the crew of the La Rochelle steam trawler Damier perished in a gale to-day, according to a wireless message received from the trawler Palombe, which was towing the Damier into port following damage she had received.

As the Damier was leaking badly, her master ordered the crew to abandon ship. The 15 hands got into a whaler, but a wave dashed the boat against the ship, throwing every occupant into the sea.

Nine of the men were picked up.—Reuter.

THE SEALS OF OFFICE

Members of the old Cabinet will be received by the King at Buckingham Palace this morning, when they will return their Seals of Office.

The Privy Council, at which members of the new Government will be sworn in and take over the seals, will follow immediately. It will take place in the Indian Room, one of the apartments on the first floor of the Palace.

NAUTILUS IN ARCTIC STORM

POUNDED BY FLOES WITHOUT

FLOOR OF ICE WITHIN

From Sir HUBERT WILKINS
(By radio)
Aboard Nautilus in Arctic Seas, Tuesday.

AS a result of our two accidents—the loss of the diving rudder and the cracking of a cell in the electric storage battery—we could not push under the ice last night.

The electric storage battery, however, has served us so exceedingly well that one cracked jar does not mean disaster. Our cells were obtained from the United States Navy and cracked jars are not infrequent happenings in the service.

With great ice cakes pounding about us, we had to make for more open water. The wind was high and the ice pack, moving fast, made the passage out difficult and slow.

WATER PIPES FREEZE

We hove near the edge of the pack this morning, hoping to submerge and steady the craft for gravity measurements. We also hoped to take deep water soundings hereabouts where the water is over 2,000 metres deep, but the storm increased, driving the ice upon us.

We had to move to open water. In the freezing cold the high wind made a misery of work on deck, from which all shelter had been removed in anticipation of the diving test.

Ice clung to the deck runners, the periscope and the top of the conning tower. Ice even formed on the floors of our living compartment, and the fresh water pipes froze solid.

To add to the discomfort, a rivet started in the diving compartment and icy water seeps slowly through.

FOG AND SNOWSTORMS

We are safe away from the edge of the heaving pack ice, whether we are in open sea or further into the floes. But so far the edge of the ice pack has been so much in motion from the wind and sea undercurrent that it has been impossible for us to go far under.

We are moving slowly up and down under the power of our electric motors. We roll heavily in a sea trough and are almost as uncomfortable as when crossing the Atlantic.

Fog and snowstorms often close right down upon us, but occasionally we see the edge of the ice pack.

To-morrow we hope for better luck and weather, so that we can push Nautilus, nose northward, under the moving ice pack.

[*Copyright by the "News-Chronicle" and King Features Syndicate. Reproduction in whole or in part prohibited.*]

2,719,376 OUT OF WORK

Official figures issued last night show that on August 17 the numbers of persons on the employment registers in Great Britain were 1,942,836 wholly unemployed, 664,801 temporarily stopped, and 111,739 normally in casual employment, making a total of 2,719,376.

This was 5,017 more than a week before and 701,419 more than a year ago.

Summer Coming Back

A WARM SPELL EXPECTED

Weather Outlook: Cool at first, then sunny and warmer.

The recent storm area has passed away across France and there is now a prospect of a general and perhaps prolonged spell of warmer and brighter weather, writes the "News-Chronicle" weather expert.

An anti-cyclone is coming in from the Atlantic and the barometer is rising generally.

The sun shone in London yesterday for several hours. If summer had been her old self that would be an obvious statement. Instead it is a statement almost unbelievable after a month or so of misplaced winter.

Here are the temperature readings taken by Messrs. Negretti and Zambra in Holborn:

	Yesterday.	Monday.
9 a.m.	55	52
1 p.m.	60	56
6 p.m.	60	55
Maximum	63	56

The maximum temperature was 7 degrees warmer than on Monday.

At Kew Observatory the temperatures for the past 11 days are the lowest since 1876.

Cattle Disease.—An outbreak of foot and mouth disease at Renhald, Bedfordshire, confirmed yesterday, was the sixth in the village in three weeks.

MAROONED MEN ESCAPE

From Our Staff Reporter
TORQUAY, Tuesday.

AFTER being marooned on lonely Thatcher rock, off Meadfoot, Torquay, since Sunday, four men on

LATE NEWS

TO-DAY'S WEATHER
Fair generally; higher day temperature

IMPREGNABLE
ELKIDE
(BRITISH MADE)
OUTLASTS THREE LEATHER SOLES
light, flexible, water-proof

Impregnable B139
The finest quality fully Chromed Box Field Boot is an outstanding example of 'Impregnable' value. Leather lined throughout, with strong double soles, it will appeal to every man who looks for a long life from his footwear.

TESTS prove that the new Elkide—obtainable exclusively on 'Impregnable' Boots and Shoes—outlasts three leather soles. Elkide is a wonderful material—light, flexible, waterproof, and very kind to your feet.
Ask to see a pair of Elkide soled 'Impregnable' at your usual shoe shop. Then try them on and begin your big footwear saving from to-day.

Guaranteed
'Impregnable' Boots and Shoes are guaranteed British-made throughout under ideal working conditions and the highest scale of wages. Separate detailed guarantees are given with 'Impregnable' Walking Footwear & 'Impregnable' Artisans' Strong Walking and Working Boots. Any 'Impregnable' Boot or Shoe can be had with the famous ELKIDE Soles.

A PAIR BOUGHT EVERY 7 SECONDS
The sales of 'Impregnable' footwear now average 1,500,000 pairs per annum. Estimated on 300 shopping days of 10 hours each in the twelve months, this works out at a pair sold every 7 seconds—a striking public testimonial to the sound quality and value of 'Impregnable' footwear.
All 'Impregnable' lines are now available in youth's sizes
Impregnabl EAS
REGISTERED
Wholesale only:
JOHN WHITE (Impregnable Boots) Ltd., RUSHDEN, N

Mr. A. Chamberlain (Admiralty). Lord Londonderry (First Commissioner of Works). Sir A. Sinclair (Scotland). Lord Amulree (Air). Sir H. Betterton (Labour). Lord Lothian (Duchy of Lancaster). Sir D. Maclean (Education). Sir J. Gilmour (Agriculture).

AUGUST

20 MONDAY   First Quarter

21 TUESDAY

22 WEDNESDAY

23 THURSDAY

24 FRIDAY

25 SATURDAY

26 SUNDAY

Daily Chronicle, Wednesday, 26 August 1931: Prime Minister Ramsay MacDonald forms a coalition government.

AUGUST ~ SEPTEMBER

---

27 MONDAY   *Summer Bank Holiday, UK (exc. Scotland)*

---

28 TUESDAY   *Full Moon*

---

29 WEDNESDAY

---

30 THURSDAY

---

31 FRIDAY

---

1 SATURDAY

---

2 SUNDAY   *Father's Day, Australia and New Zealand*

The Express on Sunday, 31 August 1997: the death of the Princess of Wales.

DIANA IS DEAD

6AM NEWS SPECIAL

rincess and odi killed in car smash

**BY JACK GEE in Paris
and JAMES EADIE in London**

NCESS Diana died last night after being
ed in a car chase in a Paris tunnel.

e suffered a fatal heart attack in hospital where
was being treated for serious injuries after being
ree from the wreckage of her mangled Mercedes.
he attack was brought on by a massive lung
orrhage. Doctors had fought for two hours to save

er boyfriend Dodi Fayed died at the crash scene,
to the River Seine.

e couple were being pursued by paparazzi at
s of up to 100 mph when their car careered into
entral reservation of a tunnel, before rolling over
al times and smashing into the tunnel wall.

ter hours of fevered speculation about the gravity
e Princess' injuries, the tragic news was confirmed
rs at the hospital.

er death was announced outside the hospital by
h Interior Minister Jean-Pierre Chevenement and
confirmed by Buckingham Palace.

rince Charles was informed immediately at Bal-
l where he broke the news to Princes William and
. Dodi's father, Mohamed Al Fayed flew to Paris
on as news of the accident broke. The 36-year-old

PAGE 3 COLUMN 6

CRASH SCENE: The wreckage of Diana's and Dodi's car in the tunnel under the Seine after the 100mph crash

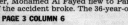

WORLD NEWS 29-31 ● OPINION 36 ● CROSSWORD 68 ● MONEY 73-80 ● TV 91-96 ● WEATHER 94

WANTED!

FOR MURDER ... FOR KIDNAPPING ..
FOR THEFT AND FOR ARSON

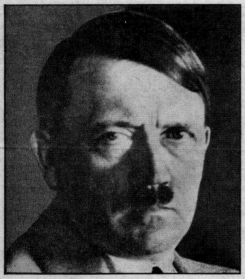

Can be recognised full face by habitual scowl. Rarely smiles. Talks rapidly, and when angered screams like a child.

ADOLF HITLER
ALIAS
Adolf Schicklegruber,
Adolf Hittler or Hidler

Last heard of in Berlin, September 3, 1939. Aged fifty, height 5ft. 8½in., dark hair, frequently brushes one lock over left forehead. Blue eyes. Sallow complexion, stout build, weighs about 11st. 3lb. Suffering from acute monomania, with periodic fits of melancholia. Frequently bursts into tears when crossed. Harsh, guttural voice, and has a habit of raising right hand to shoulder level. DANGEROUS!

Profile from a recent photograph. Black moustache. inclines to fatness. Wide nostrils. Deep-set, menacing e

FOR MURDER Wanted for the murder of over a thousand of his fellow countrymen on the night of the Blood Bath, June 30, 1934. Wanted for the murder of countless political opponents in concentration camps.

He is indicted for the murder of Jews, Germans, Austrians, Czechs, Spaniards and Poles. He is now urgently wanted for homicide against citizens of the British Empire.

Hitler is a gunman who shoots to kill. He acts first and talks afterwards.

No appeals to sentiment can move him. This gangster, surrounded by armed hoodlums, is a natural killer. The reward for his apprehension, dead or alive, is the peace of mankind.

FOR KIDNAPPING Wanted for the kidnapping of Dr. Kurt Schuschnigg, late Chancellor of Austria. Wanted for the kidnapping of Pastor Niemoller, a heroic martyr who was not afraid to put God before Hitler. Wanted for the attempted kidnapping of Dr. Benes, late President of Czechoslovakia. The kidnapping tendencies of this established criminal are marked and violent. The symptoms before an attempt are threats, blackmail and ultimatums. He offers his victims the alternatives of complete surrender or timeless incarceration in the horrors of concentration camps.

FOR THEFT Wanted for the larceny of eighty millions of Czech go March, 1939. Wanted for the armed robbery of mat resources of the Czech State. Wanted for the stealin Memelland. Wanted for robbing mankind of peace, of humanity, and fo attempted assault on civilisation itself. This dangerous lunatic masks his by spurious appeals to honour, to patriotism and to duty. At the mo when his protestations of peace and friendship are at their most veher he is most likely to commit his smash and grab.

His tactics are known and easily recognised. But Europe has already wrecked and plundered by the depredations of this armed thug who smash without scruple.

FOR ARSON Wanted as the incendiary who started the Reichstag on the night of February 27, 1933. This crime was key point, and the starting signal for a series of outr and brutalities that are unsurpassed in the records of criminal degener As a direct and immediate result of this calculated act of arson, an inn dupe, Van der Lubbe, was murdered in cold blood. But as an indirect outc of this carefully-planned offence, Europe itself is ablaze. The fires that man has kindled cannot be extinguished until he himself is apprehended— or alive!

THIS RECKLESS CRIMINAL IS WANTED—DEAD OR ALIV

All the above information has been obtained from official sources and has been collated by CASSANDRA

SEPTEMBER

---

3 MONDAY *Holiday, Canada (Labour Day) and USA (Labor Day)*

---

4 TUESDAY Last Quarter

---

5 WEDNESDAY

---

6 THURSDAY

---

7 FRIDAY

---

8 SATURDAY

---

9 SUNDAY

The Daily Mirror, Monday, 4 September 1939: the day Britain declared war with Germany.

SEPTEMBER

---

10 MONDAY

---

11 TUESDAY
New Moon

---

12 WEDNESDAY

---

13 THURSDAY

Jewish New Year (Rosh Hashanah)
First Day of Ramadân (subject to sighting of the moon)

---

14 FRIDAY

---

15 SATURDAY

---

16 SUNDAY

The Daily Telegraph, Wednesday, 12 September 2001: the terrorist attack on the
twin towers of New York's World Trade Center.

The Daily Telegraph

No 45,488   FINAL

www.telegraph.co.uk   **Britain's biggest-selling quality daily**   Wednesday, September 12, 2001   **50p**

War on America

Picture: SPENCER PLATT/GETTY IMAGES

THE United States was on a war footing last night after the most devastating terrorist attack in history.

Two hijacked passenger airliners crashed into the twin towers of New York's World Trade Centre. Both towers collapsed with the loss of thousands of lives, sending out great clouds of thick dust that covered buildings and people in the streets like volcanic ash. Lower Manhattan was evacuated and the New York skyline changed for ever.

Minutes later in Washington DC a third hijacked aircraft crashed into the Pentagon, the heart of America's military machine. A fourth, believed to be heading for the presidential retreat Camp David, crashed near Pittsburgh.

The atrocity was meticulous in its co-ordination and horrifying in its effect.

A global television audience watched in disbelief as live footage showed the second plane hitting the Trade Centre minutes after the first.

Land borders were closed and airspace cleared of all but military aircraft as US forces were put on "high alert".

Financial centres were paralysed when Wall Street closed and shares plunged across world markets. The departments of Justice, State, Treasury, Defence and the CIA were all evacuated.

President Bush was flown to a bunker in Nebraska before returning to the White House. He pledged: "Make no mistake, we will hunt down and punish those responsible for these cowardly acts."

Reports: Pages 2, 3, 4, 5, 6, 7, 8, 9 and eight-page supplement. Comment: Pages 18 & 19

The Daily Telegraph

No 45,493   FINAL

www.telegraph.co.uk

Britain's biggest-selling quality daily

Tuesday, September 18, 2001   50p

Pakistan confronts Taliban

● Opposing troops mass on Afghan border ● Bin Laden wanted dead or alive, says Bush

By Alex Spillius
IN PESHAWAR
AND ANTON LA GUARDIA
DIPLOMATIC EDITOR

PAKISTANI and Taliban forces were gathering to confront one another across the border yesterday as a final effort was made to persuade Kabul to surrender Osama bin Laden.

President Bush warned the Taliban that he wanted bin Laden "dead or alive". The Taliban leader, Mullah Mohammed Omar, said he would decide today whether to hand over the prime suspect for last week's attacks in New York and Washington.

Tens of thousands of Afghans, including members of Taliban leaders' families, were reported to be fleeing cities and towns for fear of American attacks. The Taliban threatened to retaliate against any neighbour helping the United States.

Government officials in Peshawar, capital of the North West Frontier province, said the Taliban had directed anti-aircraft guns towards Pakistan, until now their biggest backer. There were unconfirmed reports that they had also moved Scud missiles towards the border.

A Pakistani officer in the Khyber Pass, which leads from the frontier into Pakistan, said that Islamabad had reinforced its troops after the Taliban began massing forces running into thousands.

"We are forming our forces, but there has been no firing," Capt Abid Bahti said.

His comments were denied by an official military spokesman, but all the signs pointed to Pakistan gearing up to defend itself.

President Pervaiz Musharraf of Pakistan decided to support American demands for co-operation in hunting down bin Laden despite the twin threat of Taliban retaliation and a domestic backlash from Islamic groups sympathetic to the radical movement.

Anti-American demonstrations were held in four cities in Pakistan. A new coalition of Muslim parties called for nationwide protests on Friday and declared itself ready for a holy war if America attacked Afghanistan.

The Taliban's Voice of Shariat radio said Mullah Omar would announce his decision after consulting a council of clerics in Kabul.

It would be a dramatic about-turn if the movement were to sacrifice a man it has routinely described as a "guest". Repeated earlier appeals went unanswered.

President Bush adopted some of the most bellicose language used by recent occupants of the White House, comparing bin Laden to an outlaw in the days of the Wild West.

"I want justice," he said after a meeting at the Pentagon, where 188 people were killed last Tuesday when an airliner crashed into the building.

"And there's an old poster out West that says, 'Wanted: Dead or Alive'."

He seemed to temper his remarks by adding: "All I want – and America wants – is to see them brought to justice. That's what we want."

Mr Bush delivered his blunt Texas rhetoric, off the cuff, a day after Vice President Dick Cheney said that he would willingly accept bin Laden's "head on a platter".

The administration was debating whether to lift a ban on carrying out assassinations. But the White House spokesman said the directive "does not limit the United States' ability to act in self defence".

Advisers said that Mr Bush's robust rhetoric might be popular in America but would not be welcomed by European or Arab allies.

Antonio Martino, Italy's defence minister, said his country was ready to contribute troops and aircraft to an American military effort.

"We will do anything we can to participate in a response to this unacceptable, terrible act of terrorism," he said.

King Fahd of Saudi Arabia also pledged support, making clear that he wanted to dissociate his kingdom from bin Laden, who was born there.

After visiting Chancellor Schröder of Germany tomorrow evening and President Chirac of France the following morning, he will fly to Washington at Mr Bush's invitation.

On Friday he will visit New York to see the devastation caused by the suicide plane attacks before flying back to attend an emergency summit of European Union leaders in Brussels.

As investigators tried to track down a terrorist network of up to 100 people, Gen Colin Powell, the American Secretary of State, said there was growing evidence that bin Laden and his al-Qa'eda network had masterminded the devastation.

"It is becoming clear with each passing hour, with each passing day, that it is the al-Qa'eda network that is the prime suspect, as the president has said. All roads lead to the leader of that organisation, Osama bin Laden."

Mr Bush went to the Pentagon to be briefed on the call-up of reservists and plans for Operation Noble Eagle, the code-name given to the "war on terrorism" that the president has vowed to prosecute.

About 35,500 reservists were being called up for domestic protection, supporting combat air patrols over major cities and increasing staff levels at bases across the country.

With about 5,000 people confirmed dead or missing in the horrifying attacks at the World Trade Centre and the Pentagon, the United States tried to return to normality yesterday.

But nerves were on edge as John Ashcroft, the Attorney General, said associates of the terrorists who hijacked four airliners might still be at large in the country.

The Justice Department in Washington was briefly evacuated after a bomb threat and the Federal Communications Commission building was emptied while a suspect package was checked.

Shares plunge as trading restarts

By Simon English
IN NEW YORK

AMERICA'S financial centre re-opened for business yesterday for the first time since the terrorist attacks in New York and Washington forced the longest closure since the Depression.

However, the feverish activity that marked the resumption of business at the world's biggest stock market was countered by the largest one-day points fall in the Dow Jones share index.

It closed down 684·81 at 8,920·70, a fall of about 7 per cent, as investors sold shares in airlines and insurers most affected by the attacks. Some 2·4 billion shares were traded – the greatest amount ever.

Market analysts said there could be further falls today, despite an emergency interest rate cut of 0·5 percentage point – to three per cent – by the *Federal Reserve*.

Optimists said the fact that investors were able to sell indicated that there were buyers, albeit at much lower levels.

In London, the FTSE 100 index, which at one point was down 85 points, gained 143·2 to 4,898·9, closing just 35 points off its level before the terrorists struck. Stocks also rose in Frankfurt, where the Dax added 131·54 points to 4,247·52.

However, there was surprise that the Bank of England did nothing to help financial markets.

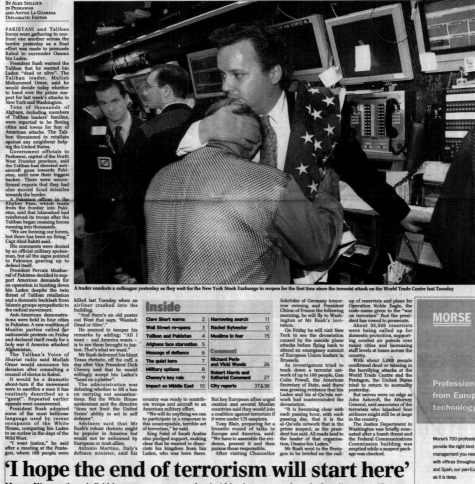

Picture: PETER MORGAN

A trader comforts a colleague yesterday as they wait for the New York Stock Exchange to reopen for the first time since the terrorist attack on the World Trade Centre last Tuesday

Inside

'I hope the end of terrorism will start here'

Marcus Warren, the only British newspaper correspondent in Afghanistan, reports from the front-line town of Bagram

THE top floor of the Bagram air traffic control tower has been holed by a shell, and a heavy machine-gun waits at the ready downstairs.

The front line in the Afghanistan civil war skirts the perimeter of this huge air base outside Kabul. To any sniper on the other side of the line, the corpulent figure of General Babajan, the local commander of anti-Taliban forces, would have made a tempting target as he lectured us on the campaign ahead.

But to us he was dramatically framed by the peaks of the Hindu Kush sheltering Kabul 22 miles to the south. And he insisted that this would be the starting point for his enemies' final defeat – with the help of the United States.

"I am a military man. I have studied the history of war," the general said. "This is not Belgium. This is not the Magi-not line. There is no demarcation zone separating two distinct countries. This is mountainous terrain and very difficult."

Even though he is a youthful 41, his nation's violent history has already given him 16 years of experience at the rank of general. And he had one piece of advice in particular for his US counterparts: if you are going to intervene here, find yourselves some good local guides.

"I know this place house by house," he said. "Compare that to some American officer who arrives here from nowhere."

He added that the airbase – the biggest in the country, and like so much of its military infrastructure a hand-me-down from the Soviet Union – could be put at the disposal of the US if Washington would co-ordinate its plans with the anti-Taliban Islamic State of Afghanistan he serves.

The runway was not as badly damaged as it might look, he said. Landing by night would be some way off but an air bridge in the hours of daylight could start when the US chose.

"I hope that the operation would start here in Bagram. If the US attacks and paralyses Kabul airport, they can begin here."

Then, Ahmad Shah Mas-soud, the commander murdered by suicide bombers linked to Osama bin Laden last weekend, would be avenged.

"I am really hopeful that the beginning of the end of terrorism will start at this very spot," Gen Babajan said, summing up. "That way will avenge the blood of Massoud and the Americans slaughtered last week."

It may, however, still take a little time. The front line was remarkably peaceful yesterday with only the occasional burst of machine-gun fire in the middle distance breaking the silence in the valley.

And yet the Taliban still control the high ground surrounded Bagram. The airbase itself is a shot-up wreck, the fire engines are burnt out and the air traffic control tower is an empty shell, equipped only with a telescope for keeping watch on the enemy.

Cars could be seen putting up clouds of dust on the Taliban side. According to the United Front, many of the Arabs and Pakistanis fighting against them have fled, but some are still travelling to Kabul and back to stock up on supplies for the onslaught ahead. Here at least the front line seems to be in a state of suspended animation.

Since the fundamentalist

Continued on Page 3

The Daily Telegraph 18-9-01

3 B

9 770307 123726

▪ A B C D E F ▪

SEPTEMBER

---

17 MONDAY

---

18 TUESDAY

---

19 WEDNESDAY   First Quarter

---

20 THURSDAY

---

21 FRIDAY

---

22 SATURDAY   *Jewish Day of Atonement (Yom Kippur)*

---

23 SUNDAY   *Autumnal Equinox*

The Daily Telegraph, Tuesday, 18 September 2001: the US government reacts to the
terrorist attacks of September 11.

SEPTEMBER

24 MONDAY

25 TUESDAY

26 WEDNESDAY   Full Moon

27 THURSDAY   *Jewish Festival of Tabernacles (Succoth), First Day*

28 FRIDAY

29 SATURDAY   *Michaelmas Day*

30 SUNDAY

Daily Express, Friday, 30 September 1938: the announcement of a peace plan between
Britain, Germany, Italy and France.

Daily Express

WORLD'S LARGEST DAILY SALE

No. 11,970   Friday, September 30, 1938   One Penny

The Daily Express declares that Britain will not be involved in a European war this year, or next year either

Agreement last night in Munich	# PEACE!	Surrender less than Hitler plan

GERMAN TROOPS IN "PEACE UNIFORM" GO IN TOMORROW

Then gradual occupation and Czech plebiscites

DUCE DRAWS FRONTIER

IT IS PEACE

AT TEN O'CLOCK LAST NIGHT HITLER, MUSSOLINI, CHAMBERLAIN, DALADIER, HELD THEIR FOURTH MEETING OF THE DAY TO SETTLE THE LAST DETAILS OF A PLAN WHICH WILL SOLVE THE CZECHO-SLOVAK PROBLEM.

Tomorrow morning, October 1, the date named in Hitler's famous "ultimatum" to the Czechs, German troops will cross the Czech frontier. But instead of steel helmets they will wear forage caps, and they will march in quietly to begin a progressive occupation of Sudetenland.

An international commission will define the new frontier; an international force, including British, French and Italian troops, will police the areas to be surrendered to Germany; doubtful zones will hold a plebiscite to decide whether they shall be German or Czech.

By October 31 the new frontier should be finally fixed and all cause for friction removed.

That is the plan; the only doubt was that the Czecho-Slovak Government might not be able to accept the plan in time. In this case London diplomats hope that Hitler might be willing to extend the time limit until Sunday.

Meanwhile there is no question of Germany ordering a general mobilisation, as threatened earlier in the week.

Mussolini is described as being particularly elated as he ordered his special train to return to Rome at midnight. A German spokesman said that a revised line of demarcation between Germans and Czechs in Hitler's map of Czecho-Slovakia was drawn by Mussolini himself.

AREA NOT SO LARGE

The area to be surrendered is not quite so large as was demanded by Hitler at Godesberg.

The German spokesman also said that the agreement provides a plebiscite for the Hungarian and Polish minorities as well as the German minority. After the plebiscite Germany will guarantee the new Czech frontier, together with other Powers.

Nazi Storm Troopers formed a cordon in the lobby of Mr. Chamberlain's Munich hotel last night. There were shouts of "Heil Chamberlain" and "Hoch Chamberlain" from the Germans when the Premier returned from the conference.

Field-Marshal Goering, in the uniform of his rank, raised a laugh in the lobby when he strolled over to the French Premier and slapped him on the back, saying:—

"Well, Herr Daladier, you had better stay here for the October Festival."

The "Oktoberfest" is Germany's great annual beer festival, which began four days ago and is still in progress.

This is the Peace Plan

By GUY EDEN,
Daily Express Political Correspondent

THIS, I understand, is the peace plan under discussion in Munich between Mr. Neville Chamberlain, Herr Hitler, Signor Mussolini, and M. Daladier, the French Premier:—

1. Handing over to Germany by tomorrow of "token" areas of the Sudetenland not vital to the defence of Czecho-Slovakia—such as the triangle formed by the towns of Carlsbad, Eger and Asch;

2. Appointment of an international commission to draw the new border-line between Germany and Czecho-Slovakia, and to see that the transfer of populations—Czechs to Czech territory and Germans to German —is carried out fairly and quietly;

3. Demobilisation of the "abnormal" rival armies on each side of the frontier, and the appointment of an international force of British, French, Italian, Belgian and Dutch troops to take over control of the areas scheduled to be ceded to Germany;

4. On stated dates, the Germans to occupy the areas under the control of the international force, the Czech troops having previously withdrawn from the area. One series of districts, it is suggested, should be given up on October 15, the second on October 31;

5. Formal settlement, on October 31, of the new frontier between Germany and Czecho-Slovakia;

6. Plebiscites to be held in other areas where there is a considerable percentage of Sudeten Germans, the vote on

➡ PAGE TWO, COL. ONE

MAP showing the areas involved ON PAGE 8

British Legion to keep peace

BERLIN, Thursday. — Well - informed sources in Berlin say that the communique is expected to provide that the British Legion shall occupy the portion of Czech territory in which the population is 40 per cent. German, while German troops will occupy territory where Germans amount to 60 per cent. or more.—British United Press.

Wall-street goes ahead

Daily Express Staff Reporter

NEW YORK, Thursday. — Encouraged by news from Munich New York's stock market advanced steadily today, prices rising one to four points.

THE PRIME MINISTER MEETS MUSSOLINI AT MUNICH. Picture wired last night; see also Back Page.

LATEST
CENTRAL 8000

SIGNED

Agreement signed in Munich at 12.30 a.m.

Weather: cooler (see page 11)

London rejoices

PREMIER'S WIFE MOBBED

CROWDS of women, rejoicing at the news from Munich, cheered Mrs. Neville Chamberlain for several minutes last night as she left St. Michael's Church, Chester-square, W., where the Archbishop of Canterbury had addressed a broadcast service.

As Mrs. Chamberlain appeared at one of the doors after the service a great crowd was waiting to cheer her. By the time her car had arrived it had grown to several thousands.

As she stepped into the car they surged round, cheering continuously.

Women with tears in their eyes grasped her hand and congratulated her on the good news.

Before the car could move away women clambered on the running boards. As they pressed forward to grasp her by the hand Mrs. Chamberlain, almost overcome by emotion, repeated "Thank you, oh, thank you."

As she drove away she smiled and waved.

DANCERS CHEER

At a Croydon theatre three thousand people cheered for nearly five minutes when the manager announced the success of the talks.

At a Streatham dance hall the news was greeted with an outburst of cheering, and the band struck up the National Anthem. Three cheers were given for the King and the Prime Minister.

People wept at the Gaiety and Princes Theatres last night, when the shows were interrupted and "Peace" was announced at 9.30.

The audiences rose and cheered and clapped for several minutes. People threw their arms round one another and women wept with relief.

Mr. Leslie Henson "broke the news" at the Gaiety.

DAILY SKETCH

No. 9,177   SATURDAY, OCTOBER 1, 1938   ONE PENNY

PREMIER SAYS 'PEACE FOR OUR TIME' – P. 3

Give Thanks In Church To-morrow

TO-MORROW is Peace Sunday.

Hardly more than a few hours ago it seemed as if it would have been the first Sunday of the most senseless and savage war in history.

The "Daily Sketch" suggests that the Nation should attend church to-morrow and give thanks.

THE fathers and mothers who might have lost their sons, the young people who would have paid the cost of war with their lives, the children who have been spared the horror of modern warfare —let them all attend Divine Service and kneel in humility and thankfulness.

To-morrow should not be allowed to pass without a sincere and reverent recognition of its significance.

MR. CHAMBERLAIN shows the paper that represents his great triumph for European peace to the thousands who gave him such a thunderous welcome at Heston yesterday. It is the historic Anglo-German Pact signed by himself and the Fuehrer Herr Hitler.

'Determined To Ensure Peace'

WHEN Mr. Chamberlain arrived at Heston last night he said:

"This morning I had another talk with the German Chancellor, Herr Hitler. Here is a paper which bears his name as well as mine. I would like to read it to you:

"'We, the German Fuehrer and Chancellor and the British Prime Minister, have had a further meeting to-day and are agreed in recognising that the question of Anglo-German relations is of the first importance for the two countries and for Europe.

"'We regard the agreement signed last night and the Anglo-German Naval Agreement as symbolic of the desire of our two peoples never to war with one another again.

"'We are resolved that the method of consultation shall be the method adopted to deal with any other questions that may concern our two countries and we are determined to continue our efforts to remove possible sources of difference and thus to contribute to the assurance of peace in Europe.'"

OCTOBER

---

1 MONDAY

---

2 TUESDAY

---

3 WEDNESDAY   Last Quarter

---

4 THURSDAY   *Jewish Festival of Tabernacles (Succoth), Eighth Day*

---

5 FRIDAY

---

6 SATURDAY

---

7 SUNDAY

Daily Sketch, Saturday 1 October 1938: Prime Minister Neville Chamberlain signs the Munich Agreement.

OCTOBER

8 MONDAY

Holiday, Canada (Thanksgiving Day)
Holiday, USA (Columbus Day)

9 TUESDAY

10 WEDNESDAY

11 THURSDAY

New Moon

12 FRIDAY

13 SATURDAY

14 SUNDAY

Daily Mirror, Saturday, 13 October 1984: the IRA bombs the Grand Hotel, Brighton, during the Conservative party conference.

DAILY Mirror

FORWARD WITH BRITAIN

October 13, 1984   ★ 16p

MURDER

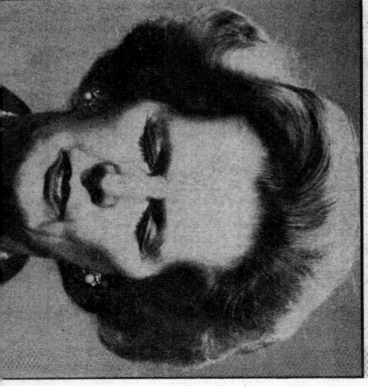

Mrs Reagan ye
bravely facing

Saturday. October 17, 1987   20p   SPORT BEGINS ON PAGE 23

BBC's bungling Michael Fish

WHY DIDN'T THEY KNOW?

At lunchtime on Thursday TV weather man Michael Fish said the would be no hurricane. B 10pm last night 18 people were dead, scores injured and the damage was £500m Why didn't the Met men know?

CRUNCH! *EastEnders* star Linda Davidson, who plays punk mum Mary, sits on her new car after it was wrecked by a falling tree outside her London home. Linda, exclusively pictured by The Sun, said: "And I've just passed my test!"   Picture: SIMON RUNTING

FULL DRAMATIC STORY: SEE PAGES 2, 3, 4, 5, and 6

OCTOBER

15 MONDAY

16 TUESDAY

17 WEDNESDAY

18 THURSDAY

19 FRIDAY   First Quarter

20 SATURDAY

21 SUNDAY

The Sun, Saturday, 17 October 1987: Britain is struck by the worst storm in 250 years.

OCTOBER

---

22 MONDAY   *Holiday, New Zealand (Labour Day)*

---

23 TUESDAY

---

24 WEDNESDAY   *United Nations Day*

---

25 THURSDAY

---

26 FRIDAY   *Full Moon*

---

27 SATURDAY

---

28 SUNDAY   *British Summertime ends*

The Evening News, Friday, 21 October 1966: a landslide from a mining waste tip engulfs the
village school in Aberfan, South Wales.

AVIA OLYMPIC
17 JEWEL SWISS LEVER SPORTS WATCHES FOR MEN AND WOMEN

World's Largest Evening Sale

The Evening News
and STAR
LONDON FRIDAY OCTOBER 21 1966

No. 26,370   HH

NIGHT SPECIAL
PRICE 4d.

MERTHYR TYDFIL

LANDDROST
FINEST MEDIUM DRY
SOUTH AFRICAN
SHERRY

A child saved. More pictures Pages Ten and Eleven.

DISASTER—a black mountain engulfs the children of Aberfan

SCHOOL TERROR —169 MISSING

'Dad, the school has been hit'

Eye-witnesses this afternoon told how they watched the mountain of slag swallow up the school of Aberfan.

Mr. George Thomas, of Aberfan Crescent, a 46-year-old miner, said he heard a terrible rumble." His son came to his bedroom and said: "The school has fallen in 'Dad."

He ran to the school. "It was as if an earthquake had happened. You could see some of the building, but the rest of it was buried," said Mr. Thomas. "It happened in a matter of minutes.

CRYING

"We found four little children underneath a lot of brickwork which had slipped down on top of them.

"One small boy was still alive. He was standing against the heater in the schoolroom and was crying because his leg had been caught in something.

"Standing by his seat were three other little children. They were dead. Several classrooms of the school collapsed, and I only saw one room which had not been too severely damaged."

Mr. Roy Parker, aged 42, steward of a village social club said he looked towards the school and "saw a wall of muck and rafters."

He added "It was as if an earthquake had struck us."

HOME ON LEAVE

Mr. Arthur Owens, a 40-year-old motor mechanic, said: "The houses fell like a pack of cards.

"We found one lady underneath the rubble, still in bed. We rescued her. We shouted to see if there were any more underneath but there was silence.

"Later we were told that there were some children in the house, together with a sailor who had come home on leave. There is no sign of them."

Mr. Owen said some rescue workers continued although they were being engulfed by the moving shale.

"The muck was coming down 40 feet high," he added. "At some places it was as high as 55 to 60 feet.

"It was as if the whole tip, which buried hundreds of feet above the village, had collapsed and moved towards the village."

SWAMPED

One woman living near the school said: "Most of the school was suddenly swamped, with little children still sitting at their desks."

Mr. Edward Jones, of Moy Road, Aberfan, said: "I heard what I thought was a clap of thunder. I went out and saw that the 'mountain' had fallen on top of the school."

One of the rescued children, six-year-old Gareth Jones, a doctor's son, said: "I was playing in the classroom when suddenly the whole wall collapsed on us.

"My teacher, Mrs. Williams, smashed a window with a brick and we climbed out. I was playing with day when there was a huge noise and atoms were falling everywhere. Some of my friends were hurt."

Champion helps in rescue

Among the rescuers were Howard Winstone, British and European boxing champion, and his manager, Eddie Thomas.

A special "Evening News" aerial view of the disaster scene showing clearly the path of destruction.

Disaster, an almost incredible disaster, overwhelmed a school with hardly a sound and without warning today.

Tonight 169 children are missing, feared dead, entombed beneath thousands of tons of rubble that engulfed them as they began their lessons.

More than 2,000,000 tons of coal dust and rubble, a black mountain towering over Pantglas mixed school in Aberfan, near Merthyr, slipped half a mile.

The disaster could be the worst accident ever in Britain involving children.

Death on a holiday

Another two-and-a-half hours and the children would have been in the safety of their homes. Half-term holiday was due to start at noon.

This evening 17 bodies had been recovered from the school, two were adults. Another five people were killed when the avalanche of mud engulfed their homes near the school.

So desperate was the rescue work that an accurate count of the casualties could not be completed.

Where 14 houses had been standing in Moy Road there was now just pieces of rubble being swept down the main street of this Rhondda village.

As rescuers fought to find life in a tangled mass the cry suddenly goes out: "Watch out, she's moving again." The huge coal heap was inching menacingly towards them.

Bulldozers tore at the wreckage and picks and shovels were handed to people in the streets.

Women prayed. Ministers and nurses helped to comfort the waiting mothers many of whom were hysterical.

School children, too, waited in silence for news of their friends.

One lucky boy . .

One of the lucky survivors was Allen Morgan, aged 14, of Aberfan Road. He was late for school and when he arrived the headmaster was outside, telling the children to go home.

Three of his friends, Robert Coffey, Raymond Collins and Andrew Rees, lay buried under the rubble.

Also lucky to escape was a middle-aged man who this morning was due to move into No. 3 Moy Road. He delayed the move by three hours, and missed being buried with his new house.

Danger acid

Firemen wearing breathing apparatus helped workmen drain a tanker containing 12 tons of hydrochloric acid into an underground tank at Tilbury generating station today, after the tanker had sprung a serious leak.

Spirits haul

Thieves broke into the premises of Hawes Brothers, wine merchants, Brent Street, Hendon, today and escaped with a large haul of whisky, gin and cigarettes.

Smash-grab raid

Smash and grab thieves escaped with radio equipment after raiding a shop in Hargrave Road, Upper Holloway today.

THE WEATHER

The Meteorological Office forecasts :

THIS EVENING : Dry. TOMORROW UNTIL MIDNIGHT : Mainly dry and sunny, but mist or fog patches morning and late afternoon, wind light and variable, near normal temperatures, maximum 14 degrees C. 57 degrees F.

OUTLOOK : Mainly dry with some sunshine, perhaps some rain later. CHANNEL : Sea slight. BAROMETER 12.0 p.m. 29.86in.

Lighting-up time 6.25 p.m. until 7.5 a.m. tomorrow. Sun sets 5.55 p.m. rises tomorrow 7.23 a.m. Moon sets 11.34 a.m. rises tomorrow 4.12 a.m. First quarter today. High water London Bridge 7.11 a.m., 7.53 p.m.

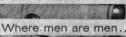

Evening Standard

42.421   WEDNESDAY, NOVEMBER 2, 1960   ●●2½d.

Jury reach historic decision after 3 hours

THE INNOCENCE OF LADY CHATTERLEY

She's cleared after 6-day trial

APPLAUSE AT OLD BAILEY

Evening Standard Reporter

Lady Chatterley's Lover is NOT obscene. So the jury at the Old Bailey decided this afternoon after being out for three hours.

There was loud clapping and applause from the back of the court when the foreman of the jury announced the verdict. Ushers cried loudly: "Silence — silence." The clapping and applause stopped.

The decided of publishing an obscene article, can go ahead with their plans to issue D. H. Lawrence's novel as a 3s. 6d. paperback.

Mr. Gerald Gardiner, QC, who had led the defence, asked for the prosecution to contribute a substantial amount towards the cost of the case. The judge refused.

Mr. Gardiner said the prosecution had been brought as a test case. It had been a decision of the Director of Public Prosecutions to obtain a decision under the new Obscene Publications Act and to see how it works.

'The American case'

Mr. Gardiner said that all the questions concerned in the case were considered "in the American case" and then it was stated that the publication of the book was not contrary to the public interest.

The costs of the six-day trial had been "very extensive."

Mr. Justice Byrne said: "I will say no more than this: I make no order as to costs."

From the court the jury went immediately to an office on the ground floor of the Old Bailey to collect their expenses. They left the court leaving behind their copies of the book which the judge had ordered them to read from cover to cover.

Meanwhile the corridor outside became crowded with people waiting to see the jurors.

But they stayed put in the office.

Words from the book

During the trial prosecuting counsel repeatedly read out "four-letter words" frequently used in the text in an effort to prove that the book would tend to deprave and corrupt young people.

The defence called 35 witnesses—they had another 36 available—to prove that Lawrence was a great novelist and that passages describing adulterous relationships would not corrupt young readers.

During his 2hr. 10min. summing-up the judge had put two questions to the jury.

1—Are you satisfied beyond reasonable doubt that the book is obscene?

2—If, upon dispassionate reading of this book, you are satisfied it is obscene, then you ask yourselves: Have the defendants established upon the balance of probability that the merits of the book as a novel are so high that they out balance the obscenity os that its publication is for the public good?

To the first question the jury answered: No.

Legally the trial was the prosecution of Penguin Books for handing a single copy of the novel—and thereby technically publishing it — to Det.-Insp. Charles Monahan, of Scotland Yard.

The prosecution—by arrangement—was to avoid individual booksellers being summoned.

There one such case in Essex recently when The   ing up . . . "The Man Behind the Scen   GE SIXTEEN.

INSIDE NEWS

Wilson Taunts Macmillan—BACK PAGE.
★ ★ ★
W. J. Brown leaves £228,766—Page NINETEEN.
★ ★ ★
Burlington Arcade Fire—Page FIVE.
★ ★ ★
Cotton's Show-Biz Plans—Page SEVENTEEN.
★ ★ ★
£250 Winners—Page NINETEEN.
★ ★ ★
Polaris Speech Surprises U.S.—Page SEVENTEEN.
★ ★ ★
Gold Reserves up £11 million—Page TWO.
★ ★ ★
Amusements Guide—Page TWENTY-TWO.

'NOW WE CAN GO AHEAD' SAYS PENGUIN CHIEF

SIR ALLEN LANE—"I feel marvellous," he said.

Evening Standard Reporter

Sir Allen Lane, head of Penguin Books, ran from the Old Bailey this afternoon after the Lady Chatterley verdict to meet a barrage of waving hands outstretched in congratulation. "I feel marvellous," he said, smiling and breathless.

Exultantly he told me: "Now we can go ahead with distributing the novel. But it will be 10 days before it is in general circulation.

"The 200,000 copies we had printed at a cost of more than £10,000 had been sent to book-shops throughout the provinces for a publication date last August."

"They had not reached London bookshops by the time it was decided to take the stock after the prosecution was launched.

Fair

"The trade was very fair and every copy we could trace came back apart from a few which went on sale accidentally in Nottingham.

"The shops they had reached were in Scotland, Northern Ireland and Northern England.

"How many copies will we print, in addition to the 200,000 now that the book has been cleared? I should think we could do with a newspaper printing press.

"We have fought the case and published the book because we felt it was right and proper to publish Lawrence's work as a whole.

"It is a big landmark in the literary education of this country."

Did he expect the result? "You can never tell with test cases like this; but I am a natural optimist—so I wasn't too surprised."

'Fresh air blows through England'

Evening Standard Reporter

Mrs. Barbara Barr, Lawrence's step-daughter, threw triumphant arms around me when she heard the news Not Guilty this afternoon at her Streatham home.

For a time she was speechless with pleasure.

Then words of joy came pouring out.

Trip to U.S.?

"I'm delighted . . . I feel as if a window has opened and fresh air blows right through England. . . Perhaps I shall fly to America to see my daughter and grandson.

"I just don't know. It's all so exciting, so sudden, so unexpected."

The question of royalties? "It is a bit early to estimate, but we might make about £5000.

"The important thing, however, is that we've won. It's a miracle."

Then she talked of what she really cared about—the fact that Lawrence's ideas of what is important — human relationship and a zest for life—should be allowed to live on through his novel.

12s. 6d. Easter egg for old folk

Evening Standard Parliamenta Reporter

An increase in the old-age pension of 12s. 6d. a week for a married couple an 7s. 6d. a week for a single person was announced by Mr. Boyd Carpenter, Minister of Pensions, in the Commons today.

The higher rates—92s. 6 for a married couple an 57s. 6d. for a single person will be payable in the first week of April Easter time.

The cost of this and other pensions increases — also announced by the Minister wi be more than £160 million a year.

Sickness benefit up

The flat-rate contributions the National Insurance scheme will have to be increased to meet the bill.

Details were being announce later today when the Bill give effect to the pension increases was being published.

The standard rate of unemployment and sickness benefit also to go up to the flat rate retirement pension level.

The standard rate of widows pension will also be raised to 57s. 6d. a week.

In the case of the widowed mother, her personal benefit will be increased to 57s. 6d. a week like other benefits, but the allowance

● Back Page, Col. Six

WEATHER—Showers.—See Page 17

OCTOBER ~ NOVEMBER

29 MONDAY   *Holiday, Republic of Ireland*

30 TUESDAY

31 WEDNESDAY   *Hallowe'en*

1 THURSDAY   *All Saints' Day*
Last Quarter

2 FRIDAY

3 SATURDAY

4 SUNDAY

Evening Standard, Wednesday, 2 November 1960: At the end of a trial under the Obscene Publications Act, *Lady Chatterley's Lover* is declared suitable for publication.

NOVEMBER

---

5 MONDAY   *Guy Fawkes' Day*

---

6 TUESDAY

---

7 WEDNESDAY

---

8 THURSDAY

---

9 FRIDAY   New Moon

---

10 SATURDAY

---

11 SUNDAY   *Remembrance Sunday, UK*
Holiday, Canada (Remembrance Day)
and USA (Veterans' Day)

The Times, Saturday, 11 November 1989: with the fall of the Berlin Wall, Germany is reunited after thirty years.

INSIDE

TRAVEL
Trekking without the cheeseburgers

BOOKS
The man who made the modern monarchy

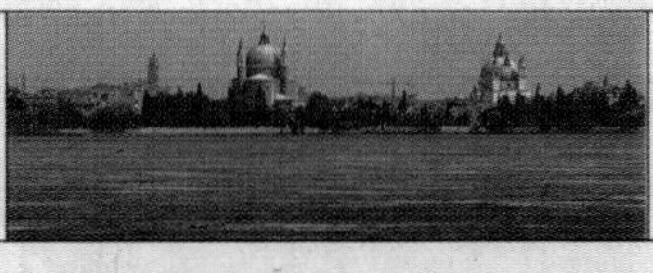

REVIEW
The last wave: would Expo sink Venice?

LAST MONTH'S AVERAGE DAILY SALE 433,000

No 63,549

THE TIMES

30p

SATURDAY NOVEMBER 11 1989

Hammering down the Wall

East German party offers free elections

From Anne McElvoy in East Berlin and Ian Murray in Bonn

East Germany's Communist Party yesterday unveiled a package of reforms including free elections, changes in the economy and parliamentary scrutiny of the security forces.

The move came as the disintegration of 40 years of Communist rule in Eastern Europe accelerated, symbolized by the East German authorities beginning to demolish 18 sections of the Berlin Wall for new crossing points.

The residents of the Eberswalderstrasse in the Prenzlauer Berg area ran to the Wall in amazement as bulldozers arrived at 9 pm to strike the first hole in the bricks that had separated them from their Western neighbours for 28 years.

As a lorry carried away the first load of rubble, hundreds of locals surged to the hole in the Wall to wave to West Berliners.

Earlier the East German Communist Party's Central Committee, ended an astonishing three-day session, by issuing an action programme. "East Germany is awakening," it said. "A revolutionary people's movement has set in motion a process of serious upheaval. The aim is dynamically to give socialism in East Germany more democracy."

The party also began an anti-corruption purge in a further attempt to bolster its waning credibility. Two leading figures from the previous Government were accused of undemocratic behaviour and incompetence.

Historic day 3
Bewildered army 3
Corruption purge 4
Impact on summit 4
Moscow warning 5
Thatcher's praise 5
John Biffen 10
Bonn's response 10
Paris response 10
Leading article 11
Shares boom 17

During another day of unprecedented upheaval, jubilant East Germans had poured through the Wall, though most intended to return to their homes. The Wall, which has divided the city since 1961, was the scene of a carnival atmosphere as Berliners held an impromptu party on and around it.

Addressing a 10,000-strong rally at the Wall last night, Herr Helmut Kohl, the West German Chancellor, said: "This is a great day for us and a great day for German history. We are and will remain one nation and we belong together. Step by step, we must find the way to our common future."

Herr Kohl had interrupted a visit to Poland to attend the rally and a Cabinet meeting today. Bonn sources said that he wanted to meet Herr Egon Krenz, the East German leader, as soon as possible.

Yesterday's historic moves came as Bulgaria's leader for the last 35 years, Mr Todor Zhivkov, resigned as head of state and Communist Party chief. The longest-serving Communist leader in Eastern Europe, he was replaced by Mr Petur Mladenov, the Foreign Minister.

Mr Zhivkov's departure leaves Mr Nicolae Ceausescu, the Romanian leader, as the last of the generation of leaders who came to power in the era immediately after Stalin.

The Soviet leadership yesterday issued a strong warning that it would not tolerate the elimination of the border between the two Germanys. Mr Gennadi Gerasimov, the Foreign Ministry spokesman, congratulated the East Germans on their decision to relax border controls. "Bonn must take into account that policies aimed at rearranging borders would not suit any government but would merely sow distrust," he said.

In contrast to the general relaxation of controls in Eastern Europe, the Kremlin last night ordered its four rebellious republics of Estonia, Latvia, Lithuania and Azerbaijan to drop laws aimed at strengthening economic and political independence.

The main problem for the West German authorities yesterday was finding accommodation for the thousands of new arrivals. However, it is a partial relief that most of the East Germans who came West early yesterday morning are going home again. "We are only here for a beer," an East German told a radio reporter in Lübeck. "Then we're off home. But we'll be back."

In West Berlin, 10,000 overnight revellers had been counted through the Wall. Only 1,000 said they intended to stay permanently. At Rudolfstein, 350 of the 1,000 who crossed registered to stay.

At the same time, people are

Continued on page 16, col 1

The Berlin Wall game: As thousands of jubilant East Berliners celebrated the end of the division of their city, a young man brought to the hated wall his own hammer to chip away at this symbol of Communist repression.

Bulgaria leader Zhivkov resigns

By Mary Dejevsky

The longest-serving leader in the Warsaw Pact, Mr Todor Zhivkov, succumbed yesterday to the accelerating pace of renewal in Eastern Europe and resigned both his official posts. Mr Zhivkov, who is 78, had been head of Bulgaria's Communist Party for 35 years and head of state since 1971.

He is succeeded as party General Secretary by Mr Petur Mladenov, aged 53, who has been Bulgaria's Foreign Minister since 1971. Mr Mladenov's long stint in foreign affairs means the complexion of his domestic political views is not known.

The announcement of Mr Zhivkov's departure came during a special meeting of the party's Central Committee in Sofia. The official news agency, BTA, said he had also asked to be relieved of his Politburo duties.

Mr Zhivkov's position has looked increasingly shaky in recent months, as change swept Hungary, Poland and even East Germany.

Two weeks ago, in what now appears as a last bid for political survival, Mr Zhivkov *issued a policy statement in* which he insisted that the Bulgarian Communist Party was still in total control.

But he admitted the severity of the economic problems facing Bulgaria, where food and consumer goods supplies to the cities have deteriorated markedly in the past two years.

Last week crowds of up to 10,000 marched through Sofia using the pretext of an authorized ecology protest to call for democracy and *glasnost*. That political demonstration, which was without precedent both in its size and the nature of its demands, indicated that Mr Zhivkov's days as leader were numbered.

NEXT WEEK

The healthy alternative?

- *The Times* Alternative Health Guide, a five-part series looking at the growing field of complementary medicine, begins on Monday
- The sixth instalment of *The Times Atlas of Ancient Civilizations* focuses on South Asia, birthplace of two great religions. It is issued free with *The Times* on Monday. Details: **Page 8**

INSIDE

- The final question in this week's competition to win a trip to Italy is on **page 34**
- There was just one winner of yesterday's £2,000 prize (see **page 7**). Today's chance to win £4,000: **Page 23**

Day trip to freedom for thousands

From Michael Binyon, West Berlin

Wild jubilation spread throughout West Berlin yesterday as thousands of East Berliners, cheering, singing and waving flags, streamed across the Wall to see for themselves the other half of a city that has been sealed off for 28 years.

Thousands of young West Berliners clambered on to the concrete wall in front of the Brandenburg Gate to look across in amazement at the lines of police who stood, revolvers firmly locked in their holsters, smiling at the young people on the Eastern side who came up to them with flowers and smiles.

Huge traffic jams built up all along the Wall as Berliners left their work to witness the amazing scenes. Many had tears in their eyes as they cheered and waved.

"I just had to come, to see the Wall now," one man said. "I don't think it will be here for much longer."

Indeed, on the Eastern side a large crane was being erected amid speculation that the East Germans would soon start to dismantle the hated concrete blocks that make up the barrier that for so long has kept families apart and symbolized a divided city and a divided Europe.

An almost carnival atmosphere reigned. East Germans wandered, dazed, being greeted spontaneously by West Berliners. "Ah, more wall-jumpers," one group of young people said.

At Checkpoint Charlie, the main crossing point from East to West Berlin, a huge crowd gathered to toast with "champagne" every East German car as it came across, in an unending stream. Thousands of people applauded and thumped on the roof of each car, crowding in upon them and shaking the hands of the families inside.

They threw rice and confetti and even the East German guards, uncharacteristically relaxed and nonchalant, managed a few smiles at the extraordinary scenes. There was also a steady stream of cars going back, much to the relief of the authorities in both halves of the city.

Many of the visitors went into the big shops of West

Continued on page 16, col 1

MPs urge rethink on power sell-off

By Philip Webster and David Young

Conservative MPs called on the Government yesterday to rethink its electricity privatization proposals in the wake of its decision to abandon the nuclear industry sale.

As Lord Marshall of Goring, chairman of the CEGB, was drawing up his letter of resignation, Mr John Wakeham, Secretary of State for Energy, was urged to consider injecting more competition by allowing at least one more generating company to rival National Power and PowerGen, which under present proposals will own all the Central Electricity Generating Board's non-nuclear power stations.

Mr Peter Rost, a senior Conservative MP who has served on the select committee on energy since 1979, said it should be announced before the flotation that National Power would be required to divest itself of about a quarter of its holdings in the next two or three years to enable another producer to enter the field.

Lord Marshall: Drawing up resignation letter.

Under the original agreement, National Power was to own 70 per cent of capacity, a high proportion to take account of the fact that it was to run the nuclear stations, and PowerGen 30 per cent. Mr Rost said yesterday: "There is now no justification for Nat-

Continued on page 16, col 8

New doctor named over kidneys sale

By David Sapsted

A third British doctor is to appear before the General Medical Council (GMC) for his alleged part in kidney operations involving impoverished Turks who were brought to London last year to sell their organs for transplant operations.

Mr Michael Joyce, a urologist at Guy's Hospital, London, and Farnborough Hospital, Kent, has not previously been named in connection with the allegations. He will appear at a disciplinary hearing next month with Dr Raymond Crockett, a Harley Street nephrologist, and Mr Michael Bewick, a leading kidney transplant surgeon.

Mr Joyce is believed to have removed the kidneys from the Turks, who were paid between £2,500-£3,260 for their organs, during operations at the Humana Wellington Hospital, north-west London. Mr Bewick is alleged to have transplanted the kidneys into wealthy foreign patients receiving dialysis under the supervision of Dr Crockett.

It is understood the charges will focus on the fact that the doctors did not satisfy themselves that the donors were not being paid or coerced into giving their kidneys to unrelated recipients.

Both Dr Crockett and Mr Bewick have denied any knowledge of or involvement in the kidney trade. Mr Joyce said at his home in Kenley, Surrey, yesterday: "As I am going before the GMC, I cannot comment."

The Department of Health ordered an inquiry and the matter was referred to the council after the extent of the trade in paid-for kidneys was disclosed in a series of articles in *The Times* earlier this year. The trade centred on a brokerage operation in Istanbul headed by Tunc Kuntar, who in the summer was sentenced to prison.

In today's Times

SECTION 1

Home news 6-8
Overseas news 3-5,9
Births, marriages, deaths 13
Church services 13
Court & Social 12
Crossword 16
Diary 10
Leading articles 11
Letters 11
Obituaries 12
On this day 13
Parliament 8
Religion 12
Television & radio 14,15
Weather 16

SECTION 2

Business news 17-21
Family Money 24-29
Stock markets 22,23

SECTION 3

Arts 41
Books 38,39
Eating Out 36
Entertainments 40
Food and drink 37
Records 42
Shopping 44,45
Week Ahead 46

SECTION 4

Sport 47-54
Law Report 54
Leisure 55
Racing 52,53
Travel 56-59

☆ ☆ ☆ ☆

C ★ ★ ★ 4

ALLIES' DRASTIC ARMISTICE TERMS TO HUNS

The Daily Mirror

CERTIFIED CIRCULATION LARGER THAN THAT OF ANY OTHER DAILY PICTURE PAPER

No. 4,696. | Registered at the G.P.O. as a Newspaper. | TUESDAY, NOVEMBER 12, 1918. | One Penny.

HOW LONDON HAILED THE END OF WAR

The King and Queen appeared on the balcony at Buckingham Palace to acknowledge the cheers of the crowd that gathered to congratulate their Majesties on the victory.

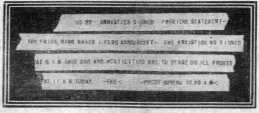

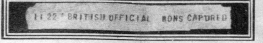

Home on short leave, but now safe for always from the dangers of Hun bullet and steel.

How news of the armistice signature came over the wire to the newspaper offices. A facsimile of it as automatically printed on the tape machine. The cheers which greeted it were the first to be raised.

An historic message as it came over the wire. It is dramatic that the last British war communiqué should proclaim our forces at Mons.

"Now entitled to rejoice" and doing it. Daddy has beaten the Huns and is coming home.

Nothing gave greater satisfaction to all of us than the news that the cessation of hostilities found the British armies once more in possession of Mons, where the immortal "Contemptibles" first taught the Huns what British valour and steadfastness could do. They left the town as defenders of a forlorn hope; they re-entered it conquerors indeed.

NOVEMBER

---

12 MONDAY

---

13 TUESDAY

---

14 WEDNESDAY

---

15 THURSDAY

---

16 FRIDAY

---

17 SATURDAY   First Quarter

---

18 SUNDAY

The Daily Mirror, Tuesday, 12 November 1918: Britain celebrates the ending of the First World War.

NOVEMBER

19 MONDAY

20 TUESDAY

21 WEDNESDAY

22 THURSDAY   *Holiday, USA (Thanksgiving Day)*

23 FRIDAY

24 SATURDAY   Full Moon

25 SUNDAY

Daily Herald, Saturday, 23 November 1963: President John F. Kennedy is assassinated in Dallas, Texas.

Daily Herald

Lawman dies too as suspect who loves Russia is seized

RUSH   252   G E RTR
DALLAS
PRESIDENT KENNEDY DEAD.
RTR. 22/11/63. IT.
THE NEWS FLASH WHICH SHOOK THE WORLD.

Lee H. Oswald (left), who was held for interrogation about the President's death.

KENNEDY ASSASSINATED

nguished Jackie cradles him in her lap

he dies

RALD REPORTER: DALLAS, TEXAS, Friday

N assassin's bullet killed resident Kennedy here afternoon, plunging world rs into turmoil.

ruck him in the head as his wife, , sat beside him in his Presidential e-domed car.

ries of shots were fired by a sniper— ably using a British rifle with a telescopic which was found in a corner window of a office block.

ent Kennedy fell face down in the back seat ar, blood pouring over his forehead.

PISTOLMAN SEIZED

guished Mrs. Kennedy cried "Oh, no!" Week- knelt down on the floor of the car and cradled g husband's head in her lap.

r bullet had struck Governor John Connally, of ne was sitting on the other side of the President. wounded in the chest and was tonight reported to al."

urs after the assassination, police seized 24-year- . Oswald as the suspected killer. The arrest cost fe—that of a policeman who was shot at a cinema o which he had tracked Oswald.

saw Oswald dragged from the cinema, brandish- tol. A policeman quoted him as saying: "Well, it's now."

lice had difficulty in holding back the crowd, y intent on a lynching, as Oswald was hurried off aarters to be grilled by FBI agents.

ld has a Russian wife—and four years ago, reported, he went to Russia as a tourist and the American Embassy there he was applying Soviet citizenship.

assination took place as the President's car entered underpass on his way from Love Airport to the rt in Dallas, where Mr. Kennedy was to have made

s on a vote-catching swing through the Deep ying to stem the mounting criticism of his racial on policy.

is the stronghold of Senator Barry Goldwater, expected to be Kennedy's Republican rival when up for re-election next November.

ecret Service agents, crushing the chaos that in the Presidential motorcade when the shots were wed the President's car to a road leading to the Hospital, not far from the Trade Mart.

CALL FOR PRIEST

esident was still lying flat on his face in the car pulled up within five minutes at the hospital y entrance. Mrs. Kennedy was weeping, with her er hands, and her clothes covered in blood.

esident was unconscious as he and Governor were hurried to an emergency treatment room. wards, Governor Connally was moved to an theatre.

blood transfusion equipment was rushed to the e beside a call went out for a priest. It was at the President was dying.

ests dashed to the emergency room to give him

The President falls forward—Jackie lets out a cry of anguish and grabs him crying "Oh, no!"

the last rites of the Roman Catholic Church and to share Mrs. Kennedy's ordeal at his bedside.

Twenty-five minutes after his admission the President was dead. It was just after 1 pm.

A priest came out of the emergency room and thrust his way past the barrier of police and Secret Service agents holding back the host of reporters who accompany the President everywhere.

It was he who broke the news. Among those who heard it from him was Vice-President Lyndon Johnson, who automatically succeeds Mr. Kennedy in the White House.

Mr. Johnson assumed the full constitutional responsibilities of the Presidency immediately on the death of Mr. Kennedy

He took his oath of office aboard the Presidential plane while it stood at Love Airport preparing to fly to Washington.

Tears streamed down his face as he was sworn in by U.S. District Judge Sarah T. Hughes as the 36th President of the U.S.

Back at the Parkland Hospital the President's body was being removed in a tightly-curtained cream ambulance. He was on his final journey to Washington aboard the same plane as President Johnson. Mrs. Kennedy was with him. She appeared dazed and in a state of shock.

Doctors said the President died of wounds in the neck and head. They were possibly caused by the same bullet, but there might have been two bullets.

He never regained consciousness from the moment he was struck, they said.

The horror of the assassination was mirrored in an eyewitness account by Senator Ralph Yarborough, Democrat, Texas, who had been riding three cars behind Kennedy.

"You could tell something awful and tragic had happened," the senator told reporters before Kennedy's death became known.

His voice breaking and his eyes red-rimmed, Yarborough said: "I could see a Secret Service man in the President's car leaning on the car with his hands in anger and anguish and despair.

GUARD LOOPHOLE

"I knew then something tragic had happened."

"The President, hatless as usual, had been waving to the cheering throng when the bullet passed through his head."

Said a man who was 15ft. away: " An awful look crossed his face and he collapsed in the car."

The assassin had taken advantage of a rare loophole in the security ring around the President. There was no guard on the underpass when the shooting took place, though Dallas abounds with fervid opponents of the President's Civil Rights policy.

They have divided the ranks of the Texas Democrats, and the President had gone to Texas to try to unify them again in the face of the coming election.

By W. N. EWER
Herald Diplomatic Correspondent

THE death of President Kennedy is a political, as well as a personal, shock to all Governments all across the world.

Suddenly one of the key figures of world affairs has been removed. There is a sense of vacuum. No one can foresee the effects.

The President of the United States, whoever he may be, is the head of the greatest of world powers.

And John Kennedy, young though he was, had already made his mark as a great President.

He had shown both courage and cool judgment in acutely difficult situations.

Cuba was his greatest test. Perhaps his "finest hour."

He had established a personal authority and influence over and above that of his great office.

RESPECT

He had earned the respect of Mr. Kruschev. That direct line between the Kremlin and the White House, suggested by the President and agreed to by Mr. Kruschev, was a symbol of a new relationship.

In the Western Alliance his position was unique. Not only because the United States is, inevitably, a predominant partner." But because of his own personality.

Whatever difficulties and differences might arise there was, among all America's allies, the feeling that one could "trust John Kennedy."

And there was an increasing respect for his judgment. His views on any problem had come to have an authority of their own.

A VOID

Now all that has vanished. where there was a great President, a great individual factor in world politics, there is a sudden void.

It will be filled. And all statesmen in all countries will wish well to Mr. Lyndon Johnson, called so suddenly and tragically to the vast responsibilities of the Presidency.

But for the moment there is in addition to the sense of personal loss, a sense of anxiety.

The passing of John Kennedy is bound to make a difference. Not a fundamental one. The United States is greater than any President. But still a difference. There is a new uncertainty in an uncertain world.

The shooting—before and after . . . Page Two.

The boy, the man, the President . . . Page Three.

The life of John Kennedy . . . Page Six.

DAILY Mirror

Thursday, November 29, 1990 **BRITAIN'S TOP COLOUR NEWSPAPER** Sale w/e November 10: 3,820,329 (INCORPORATING THE DAILY RECORD) 25p

Sad Thatcher's final farewell to No 10

TEARS IN THE BACK SEAT

MARGARET Thatcher weeps as she leaves the base of all her power – the "flat over the shop" at No 10 Downing Street. The Iron Lady's eyes filled with tears, and she bit her lip, as she hunched forward in her car yesterday for one last look at home.

Then, with faithful Denis at her side, she settled down to

EXCLUSIVE picture by KEN LENNOX

her new role as a back seat driver. The outgoing Premier had kept her composure as she spoke outside No 10 "11½ wonderfully happy years." But the bitter end quickly followed.

● Hello, No 11 – Page 4

NOVEMBER ~ DECEMBER

26 MONDAY

---

27 TUESDAY

---

28 WEDNESDAY

---

29 THURSDAY

---

30 FRIDAY   *St Andrew's Day*

---

1 SATURDAY   Last Quarter

---

2 SUNDAY   *Advent Sunday*

Daily Mirror, Thursday, 29 November 1990: the outgoing Prime Minister, Margaret Thatcher, leaves No. 10 Downing Street.

DECEMBER

---

3 MONDAY

---

4 TUESDAY

---

5 WEDNESDAY   *Jewish Festival of Chanukah, First Day*

---

6 THURSDAY

---

7 FRIDAY

---

8 SATURDAY

---

9 SUNDAY   *New Moon*

The Daily Mirror, Tuesday, 5 December 1916: the Antarctic explorer, Sir Ernest Shackleton, rescues his expedition comrades from Elephant Island.

TWO DAYS FOR RECONSTRUCTION OF CABINET—COMMONS ADJOURN

The Daily Mirror

CERTIFIED CIRCULATION LARGER THAN THAT OF ANY OTHER DAILY PICTURE PAPER

No. 4,093. | Registered at the G.P.O. as a Newspaper. | TUESDAY, DECEMBER 5, 1916 | One Halfpenny.

ONE OF THE MOST HEROIC RESCUES IN HISTORY: SIR ERNEST SHACKLETON'S 750-MILE VOYAGE IN A SMALL BOAT.

No writer of books of adventure has ever conceived such a wonderful story as that of Sir Ernest Shackleton's voyage across the Atlantic from Elephant Island to South Georgia. Four days after the expedition had landed he left in a small boat with five volunteers—Captain Worsley, Tom Crean, MacNish, Vincent and McCarthy—to seek aid for his comrades, and here the party is seen setting out on its perilous voyage.

"We decked her with sledge runners, box lids, and canvas, and made her as seaworthy as we could, but she seemed a crazy craft in which to sail 750 miles through the ice and gales," said Mr. MacNish in relating their adventures. The journey, he remarked, was almost worse than anticipated, and the greatest handicap was the ice, which formed on the boat. One man was constantly employed in cutting it away with an axe.

After being driven out of the ice hole, the party lived on this inhospitable spot on Elephant Island until rescued by Sir Ernest. In the background are glaciers from which avalanches were always threatening to break away and fill the bay and, by the waves created, to sweep them off the spot. Here some of the explorers are seen skinning Gento penguins, their principal food for four and a half months. All the photographs of the expedition appearing in this issue are exclusive to The Daily Mirror.

JOHN LENNON shot dead in New York Dec 8 1980

DEATH OF A HERO

MURDERED SUPERSTAR: One of the last pictures of ex-Beatle John Lennon, taken in New York three wee

Please turn to Pages Two and Three

DECEMBER

10 MONDAY

11 TUESDAY

12 WEDNESDAY

13 THURSDAY

14 FRIDAY

15 SATURDAY

16 SUNDAY

Daily Mirror, Wednesday, 10 December 1980: Beatle John Lennon is shot dead in New York.

DECEMBER

17 MONDAY   First Quarter

---

18 TUESDAY

---

19 WEDNESDAY

---

20 THURSDAY

---

21 FRIDAY

---

22 SATURDAY   *Winter Solstice*

---

23 SUNDAY

The Sun, Wednesday, 23 December 1992: the Queen refers to her 'annus horribilis' in her
Christmas Day broadcast to the nation.

THE Sun

25P
A CRACKER AT THE PRICE

y, December 23, 1992   25p   Today's TV: Pages 20 and 21   Audited daily sale for November 3,515,236

Sun WORLD EXCLUSIVE

OUR DIFFICULT DAYS, BY THE QUEEN

er Christmas TV message
lls of the Royal crisis year

By JOHN KAY

THE QUEEN will pour out her anguish over the Royals' problems when she speaks to the nation on Christmas Day. In an emotional address recorded yesterday, she talks of the "difficult days" she has lived through in 1992.

She admits there is no miracle solution for transforming sorrow into happiness. But she holds out hope that 1993 will be a better year for the Royals and for th rest of the United Kingdom.

In an unprecedented coup, The Sun obtained a tape of the Queen's address within hours of it being recorded. It will go out on television and radio on Friday to a worldwide audience of more than 100million.

It is the first time a full transcript of the Queen's Christmas Day message has been published in advance. The address underlines the 66-year-old Queen's recent speech in which she referred to 1992 as her "annus horribilis."

The "horrible year", her 40th on the throne, included the breakdown of the marriages of both Prince Charles and Prince Andrew, Princess Anne's divorce from Mark Phillips, and the £100million Windsor Castle fire.

In her address, the Queen says: "Like many other families, we have lived through some difficult days this year.

"The prayers, understanding and sympathy given to us by so many of you in good times and bad have lent us great support and encouragement.

ROCKED

"It has touched me deeply, but much of this has come from those of you who have troubles of your own.

"As some of you may have heard me observe, it has been a sombre year."

Her Majesty does not mention the separation of Charles and Diana and the split between Andrew and Fergie.

But it is clear they are uppermost in her mind.

During the year, the Royals were also rocked by tapes of intimate chats between Di and her close friend James Gilbey, and

The Queen . . . hopes '93 will be better year

Continued on Page 14

Daily Mail

FOR KING AND EMPIRE

NO. 13,941 ** TUESDAY, DECEMBER 31, 1940 ONE PENNY

LATE WAR NEWS SPECIAL

WAR'S GREATEST PICTURE: St. Paul's Stands Unharmed in the Midst of the Burning City

ROAR of gun barrage mingled with roar and crackle of flames; raiders droned overhead. Daily Mail cameraman H. A. Mason stood on a City roof to get this awe-inspiring picture of the second Great Fire of London—St. Paul's Cathedral ringed with flame. "I focussed at intervals as the great dome loomed up through the smoke," he said. "Glare of many fires and sweeping clouds of smoke kept hiding the shape. Then a wind sprang up. Suddenly the shining cross, dome, and towers stood out like a symbol in the inferno. The scene was unbelievable. In that moment or two I released my shutter." Here is his picture, one that all Britain will cherish—for it symbolises the steadiness of London's stand against the enemy: the firmness of Right against Wrong.

. Other pictures showing the raid havoc are in the BACK Page.

Hitler Planned Monday Swoop

London was to Blaze First

By NOEL MONKS, Daily Mail Air Correspondent

HITLER meant to start the second Great Fire of London as the prelude to an invasion.

This was the belief held in well-informed quarters in London yesterday.

The Nazis planned to set big fires burning all over London before midnight.

Relays of bombers laden with H.E. would then have carried out the most destructive raid of the war. The New Year invasion was to have followed.

The R.A.F. have given more attention to the invasion ports this past week than for two months or more. Clearly there are sound reasons for supposing that Hitler is still going ahead with invasion plans.

THE FACTS

Here are the real facts of Sunday night's fire-raising raid, as told to me yesterday:

It was one of the biggest night attacks on Britain since September.

No R.A.F. night fighters were operating over the London area, though some were doing so between London and the coast.

Soon after 10 p.m. the German Air Command sent out instructions for all the bombers then engaged to return to their bases, as the weather had taken a turn for the worse and fog was blotting out their aerodromes.

It was the weather, then, and not our night fighters, that saved London from an even worse attack. The view is held that the assault was intended to be the fiercest of the war.

Up to 1,000 bombers were to have been used during the night.

One explanation given for the sudden silence of London's inner A.A. barrage is that in the light of the fire by which most of London was lit up, to continue firing would have disclosed the positions of the guns.

Some of the German fighter-bombers came down to a lower height over London than ever before. They were able to do this because:

(i) The guns had stopped firing, and

(ii) Flames lit up the barrage balloons, and the raiders could fly between them.

It is estimated that more than 10,000 incendiary bombs were dropped on the capital within three hours.

Until a late hour last night no raids had been reported from any part of Britain.

Because of bad weather across the Channel most of the R.A.F.'s operations on Sunday night had to be cancelled.

Churchill Sees London's Ruins

MR WINSTON CHURCHILL, accompanied by his wife, visited the ruins of London's famous Guildhall yesterday and spent two hours walking through the City.

As they walked along people cheered. One man shouted, "God bless you, sir." Mr. Churchill smiled and lifted his hat.

They inspected a deep, underground shelter. To shouts of "Good luck" from the crowd, Mr. Churchill replied, "Good luck to you."

As they left this shelter a woman ran forward and asked: "When will the war be over?"

Mr. Churchill paused, turned to the woman, and said, "When we've beaten em."

Mr. Churchill looked grim and determined as he noted the damaged churches and other buildings.

The news of his visit spread, and after a while a crowd of cheering Londoners were accompanying him on his tour.

Morrison on Radio To-night

MR. HERBERT MORRISON, Minister of Home Security, will broadcast after the B.B.C.'s six o'clock news bulletin this evening.

He will detail further measures being taken to assist fire fighting during air raids, and it is believed that he will deal with the need for greater fire-watching precautions at unoccupied or temporarily unoccupied business premises.

HAVOC COULD HAVE BEEN SAVED

By Daily Mail Reporter

MANY of Sunday night's fires in the City of London could have been avoided if fire-watching regulations had been properly observed.

That is the opinion of Commander A. N. G. Firebrace, the London Fire Brigade chief, who has just been transferred to the Home Office to help in organising local brigade duties through the country.

"It should be a point of honour," he declared, "for every firm to say: 'I will not let this place burn down, both for my own sake and for the sake of my neighbours.'"

Commander Firebrace was present at an urgent conference called yesterday by Mr. Herbert Morrison at the Home Office to consider the problems arising out of the fires.

Others present were Sir Philip Game, Commissioner of Police for the Metropolis, General Sir William Bartholomew, chief of civil defence for the London area, and A.R.P. experts.

Even on Sundays

The whole available details of the raid were reported to Mr. Morrison, who will broadcast this evening during the 6 o'clock news.

The work of the firemen on duty throughout Sunday night was directed personally by Mr. F. W. Jackson, now in charge of the London Fire Brigade.

Mr. Jackson was having a brief holiday about 50 miles away from London when news of the raid reached him. He drove at once to London at the fullest possible speed, and was on duty all night.

Here is what another of Britain's fire-fighting experts said about the absence of spotters:

"If a proper fire-watching staff had been on duty at all the buildings affected nearly all the fires would have been prevented.

"It is terrible to see a little fire start, and then in half an hour to see the whole roof ablaze.

"What is needed is not merely one roof-spotter—you want a man on watch on the roof and then a party of half a dozen or so below who can be called up at once in an emergency.

"Employees of the various firms should in every case form a rota and stay behind—even on Sundays—so as to ensure that their building cannot be destroyed by a few small incendiary bombs."

The Second Great Fire of London, and Where Were the Roof Spotters?—Page THREE. Pictures—BACK Page.

'Spain to Fortify Canary Islands'

Daily Mail Radio Station

General Franco has signed a decree providing for the fortification of the Canary Islands, according to a Moscow report quoted by the Belgrade radio last night.

Berlin Radio Went 'All Quiet'

Berlin radio eliminated all reference to the destruction of churches and historic buildings in its broadcast account last night of the fire raid on London. Neither did it follow its usual practice of giving interviews with raiding pilots.

Bremen Radio's English announcer described it as a fierce mass attack, concentrated in the space of a few hours.

"A great number of fires were caused in a relatively small space," he said, "although the attack was pressed home with strong formations it came as a surprise to the enemy, and the German Luftwaffe sustained no losses."

No reference was made to the whereabouts of the fires other than "the eastern part of London."—B.U.P.

'Four Raiders in Pacific'

Daily Mail Radio Station

Four German raiders are now operating in the Pacific between Australia and China, states a Shanghai report quoted by the Moscow radio.

Up to date, it was asserted, 13 ships have disappeared in those waters. The ships have been of British, Dutch, and Norwegian nationality.

100 to 1 Backing for Roosevelt

From Daily Mail Corresponden

WASHINGTON, Monday.

PRESIDENT ROOSEVELT is "tremendously pleased" at the reaction to his speech, in which he pledged more aid to Britain and declared that the Axis could not win the war.

The President's secretary, Mr. Stephen Early, said to-day that the address had brought a greater response than any previous Roosevelt talk.

Within 40 minutes of its end the President received 600 messages. They were 100 to 1 in favour.

This is how it was received by:

Senator Alben Barkley, leader of the Democratic Party in the Senate: A magnificent clarification of our objectives.

Senator Warren R. Austin, leader of the Republican Party Minority in the Senate: A remarkably fine presentation of the situation.

The New York Sun: Deadly, implacable hostility towards the dictatorships sounded in every phrase.

New York Post: One of the major declarations in the history of our republic. It may still save our peace and our world.

'End of Hitler'

Ralph Ingersoll, editor of P.M.: The end of Hitler is very near now. If he thinks he has a chance after Roosevelt's speech last night, he is even crazier than he sounds.

Mr. Arthur Purvis, head of the British Purchasing Mission in the United States, attended a conference at the White House to-day with President Roosevelt and Mr. Henry Morgenthau, Secretary of the Treasury, on the production of material for Britain.

"We had a general discussion on supply matters," Mr. Purvis said later. "President Roosevelt's loan and lease plan opens up a new chapter."

China Seeks U.S. Planes

From Daily Mail Correspondent

NEW YORK, Monday. — The United States Government are reported to be considering the release of 400 warplanes to China for use against the Japanese.

Major-General San-chu Mow, head of the Chinese Air Force, is in Washington conferring with Administration officials and Army and Navy leaders.

Some of the foremost American strategists favour the transfer of at least 400 of the latest type pursuit and bomber planes, including six Flying Fortresses.

According to a *Reuter* report from Chungking, the Anglo-Chinese short-term credit guarantee agreement has been extended for six months to facilitate Chinese purchases from Great Britain.

500 Were Killed in Manchester

Mr. R. H. Adcock, Manchester's Town Clerk, revealed last night that in the severe raids on the city a week ago, about 500 people were killed.

He made the statement to check rumours. In one case it was rumoured that hundreds were killed in a shelter, when in fact only a few were injured.

America Moves

BIG ARMS FLOW HAS BEGUN

From Daily Mail Correspondent

NEW YORK, Monday.

THE United States Defence Commission announced to-day that they had approved arms contracts worth £2,500,000,000.

Monthly production had now risen to 2,400 aircraft engines, 700 warplanes, 100 tanks, and 10,000 automatic rifles.

Present British and American orders on hand total 50,000 planes, 130,000 aero-engines, 9,200 tanks, 2,055,000 guns, 380 naval vessels, 200 merchant ships, 50,000 lorries, and other equipment.

The United States Government were building 40 war factories, including the first plant for mass-producing tanks.

LATEST

MORE U.S. AID FOR GREECE

Washington, Monday. Mr. Morgenthau, Secretary of the Treasury, indicated to-day that President Roosevelt may extend his "loan or lease" plan to Greece and China, in addition to Britain. —Exchange.

ADMIRAL LEAHY REACHES EUROPE

Vichy, Monday. — Admiral Leahy, the new American Ambassador to the French Government at Vichy, has arrived in Lisbon on board the United States cruiser Tuscaloosa, states a Havas despatch.—Reuter.

DECEMBER

---

24 MONDAY

Christmas Eve
Full Moon

---

25 TUESDAY

Christmas Day
Holiday, UK, Republic of Ireland, Canada,
USA, Australia and New Zealand

---

26 WEDNESDAY

Boxing Day (St Stephen's Day)
Holiday, UK, Republic of Ireland, Canada,
Australia and New Zealand

---

27 THURSDAY

---

28 FRIDAY

---

29 SATURDAY

---

30 SUNDAY

Daily Mail, Tuesday, 31 December 1940: a German air raid destroys buildings in the City of London, leaving St Paul's Cathedral unharmed.

DECEMBER ~ JANUARY

---

31 MONDAY

New Year's Eve
Last Quarter

---

1 TUESDAY

New Year's Day
Holiday, UK, Republic of Ireland, Canada,
USA, Australia and New Zealand

---

2 WEDNESDAY

Holiday, Scotland and New Zealand

---

3 THURSDAY

---

4 FRIDAY

---

5 SATURDAY

---

6 SUNDAY

Epiphany

The Guardian, Friday, 1 January 1999: eleven European Union member states adopt the euro as their common currency.

45p
Friday
January 1
1999
Published in London
and Manchester

The Guardian

NEWSPAPER OF THE YEAR

| Austria | Belgium | Finland | France | Germany | The Netherlands | Ireland | Italy | Portugal | Spain |

Welcome to Euroland

Britain on sidelines as 300m people in 11 states launch single currency

Alex Brummer, Mark Milner and Martin Walker in Brussels

EUROPE today took its boldest step towards integration when 11 states scrapped centuries of history to adopt the euro as their common currency.

Euroland, as the new currency bloc is known, will be one of the world's economic powerhouses, embracing more than 300 million people and responsible for one fifth of the world's output — not far behind the United States.

The arrival of the euro is emblematic of Europe's 50-year drive to bury the ghost of two world wars and usher in a period of harmony and stability based on common economic interests and developing political and defence ties. It grows out of the ideals established by the Treaty of Rome in 1957.

Amid the elan, enthusiasm and balloons which attended the birth at a champagne reception in Brussels yesterday, there were still shadows over the project. Notably absent from the party was the Chancellor, Gordon Brown — Britain remains outside Euroland — and there was bickering about the future leadership of the all-powerful European central bank.

The German chancellor, Gerhard Schröder, was quick to endorse the single currency, in which his country will play the anchor role. "Our future begins on January 1 1999: the euro is Europe's key to the 21st century. The era of solo national fiscal and economic policy is over," he said. His paean to the euro contrasts markedly with his views as recently as March 1998, when he characterised it as a "sickly premature infant", the result of an "overhasty monetary union".

The European Commission president, Jacques Santer, registered the importance of the currency, saying: "The euro is now in your hands. It belongs to you, citizens of Europe. It is in your interests

'Our future begins on January 1 1999: the euro is Europe's key to the 21st century. The era of solo national fiscal and economic policy is over'

German chancellor Gerhard Schröder

to use it and give it life."

Wim Duisenberg, president of the new European central bank, commented: "The euro is far more than a medium of exchange . . . It is part of the identity of a people. It reflects what they have in common now and in the future."

But even as the euro was launched Mr Duisenberg had to defuse a row with the French government over when he would quit as president of the ECB to make way for France's Jean-Claude Trichet.

The launch of the euro came into effect at midnight last night, after European finance ministers had set the rates at which national currencies are now "locked" into the euro. One euro will initially be worth 70p.

Although notes and coins will not circulate until 2002, and British membership

remains in abeyance, UK business instantly adapted to the new regime. From today British Airways passengers flying to and from Europe will be offered the option of paying in euros. Marks & Spencer stores will be fully equipped to accept euros, and building societies and banks are offering euro savings accounts and mortgages.

When financial markets reopen for full-scale trading on January 4, after the New Year holiday, some 9,951 financial institutions from Helsinki to Rome and from Dublin to Vienna will be engaged in a spider's web of transactions, using the euro. The first foreign exchange trades in the euro will take place in Australasia on Sunday night.

The City of London, the world's biggest foreign exchange market, will start to trade in euros in the early hours of Monday morning. Shares in leading European bonds and sophisticated financial instruments will be quoted in euros.

Many corporations, including some British firms like ICI, will be invoicing in the currency. Some 60 per cent of shares traded in London are in foreign companies, many of them European.

Some 30,000 City staff will be at work today as the financial community begins the task of switching its systems from trading in the 11 member currencies to the euro.

City restaurants and wine

bars will be open, tons of freshly made sandwiches are being shipped into the Square Mile, and London Underground will open the special line which moves thousands of commuters from Waterloo to Bank station, in the heart of the City. Some 3,500 free parking spaces are being allocated, and banks have block-booked hotel rooms.

More than one-third of the world's foreign exchange transactions are conducted by the British banks and the 500 foreign institutions across the City — six times more than in Frankfurt, the home of the European central bank.

The 11 Euroland countries — Germany, France, Italy, Spain, Portugal, Belgium, the Netherlands, Luxembourg, Austria, Ireland and Finland — come together at a fortuitous juncture. Inflation across the 11 slipped below 1 per cent in November, down from 1.7 per cent a year earlier. The gap between the highest and the lowest inflation countries has narrowed considerably, which may make it easier for investors to accept the euro as a serious rival to the dollar.

There is a general expectation that when full-scale trading starts the euro could initially rise against the dollar, the yen and the pound.

Birth of euro, page 3; Paul Lashmar, page 14; Letters and Leader comment, page 18; Notebook, page 16; London weighs risks, page 17

The face of a euro is unveiled in Paris while, above, the euro coins of the participating countries are shown. The coins will not come into use for three years. Belgium and Luxembourg will share the same coin   MAIN PHOTOGRAPH: MAL LANGSDON

MM minus I bugs Roman scholars

Julian Borger in Washington

WHILE the pundits have been wringing their hands over Y2K — the prospect of a computer meltdown in 2000 — they have somehow allowed another quandary, brewing since Roman times, to creep up. Is this the first day of MCMXCIX, MDCCCCLXXXXVIIII, or just MIM?

There seems to be no consensus on how to write 1999 in Roman numerals, leaving architects, librarians, Olympic organisers and the people who do the rolling

credits at the end of movies stuck for a definitive answer.

Even the US National Institute of Standards and Technology, the arbiter of most time-oriented problems with all its scientists and nuclear clocks, admits it is baffled.

A spokesman for the institute, Michael Newman, conceded yesterday: "We got a question about this some time ago and some researchers have been working on it, but there is no one answer.

"Romans did not use subtraction like we do now — IX for 9 for example. So they would have spelt it the long

way: MDCCCCLXXXXVIIII. We felt MCMXCIX tends to follow the 20th century tradition."

But what about the modishly compact MIM? Mr Newman said it got the thumbs-down for not being sufficiently posh.

"I don't think MIM will get used all that much. It looks a little dinky. If you're using Roman numerals, you probably want it to look impressive."

Part of the problem is that the Romans never came up with a figure for zero — that was left for Arab mathematicians. But despite its obvious advantages, the Arab system did

not supplant Roman numerals until the 16th century. And even four centuries later, the Roman style retains a certain kudos.

The Institute of Standards freely admits to having been blind-sided by the problem, as it had been focusing on the burning issue of when the new millennium really starts — January 1 2000, or a year later. At least, Mr Newman pointed out, the MIM crisis is unlikely to prove as catastrophic as Y2K, or should that be YMM?

Millennium bug could close schools, page 9; End of world very nigh indeed, page 10

How Harold Wilson aimed to ban foreign holidays

HAROLD Wilson's Labour government drew up a secret plan in 1968 to ban foreign holidays and restrict luxury imports in a bid to save the economy, cabinet papers released today reveal.

Under the plan, imports of French wine, Swiss chocolate, avocados and out of season strawberries would have been limited in the event of a "major external cataclysm". Wilson and his colleagues agonised over the inclusion of tinned salmon on the list.

The plan, never implemented, was overseen by the then chancellor, Lord Jenkins. Only the prime minister and a handful of cabinet ministers were aware of it.

The fingerprints of MI5 can be found throughout the documents released today, as Wilson's government struggled with internal splits, leaks and street protests.

MI5 conducted a leak inquiry into Guardian journalist Ian Aitken and Financial Times reporter John Bourne over cabinet split stories. It also provided lurid briefings about the influence of "extremists" in demonstrations, and reported that what had been regarded as spontaneous marches by dockers backing Enoch Powell had been organised by the far right.

Full reports, pages 4-5; Leader comment, page 15

Inside

Home	**International**	**Finance**	**Sport**
The hostages who survived the bloody gun battle in the Yemeni desert began their journey back to Britain.	Muscovites rushed to buy presents, champagne and vodka, despite the expectation of three-figure inflation in 1999.	Eight of Britain's largest building societies face a battle over their future after being targeted by rebel members.	England countered the recall of Shane Warne by summoning Ashley Giles for their 5th Test squad in Sydney. Sport99
7	**12**	**16**	**4**

Weather 11; Obituaries 13
Comment 14; Crossword 18
Friday Review
Television and radio for
New Year's Day 18-19

53

9 770261 307354

NOTES